easy chinese food
anyone can make

easy chinese food
anyone can make

Interlink Books
An imprint of Interlink Publishing Group, Inc.
Northampton, Massachusetts

contents

introduction — 6

basic pantry ingredients — 10
specialty ingredients — 14
how to cook perfect rice — 18
how to steam things — 20
chinese dining etiquette — 22

whip up on a weeknight	24
fried rice 5 ways	54
takeout at home	60
noodles 5 ways	94
easy weekend winners	100
dumplings + wontons	134
sides + snacks to share	154
sauces + condiments	184
desserts	192

index	216
conversion tables	219
thanks	222
about the author	223

introduction

In Mandarin, we use the term *jiā cháng cài* 家常菜 to describe homestyle cooking. This type of food is unpretentious, delicious and deeply intertwined with the comfort of being at home. Having spent many years living abroad, this is the type of food I crave when I'm homesick. I don't believe you need lots of time, money or equipment to make delicious Chinese food. That's why this book is a collection of recipes that are easy, approachable and adaptable. Recipes that ANYONE, even those with limited time, space, budget or even cooking skills, can make at home.

My goal was to make this book as accessible as possible for the modern, everyday cook, while making sure the recipes still feel authentic to me. The result is a book filled with the foods and flavors I grew up enjoying in Hong Kong and Shanghai. You'll find quick recipes that I cook on busy weeknights, as well as larger, family-style dishes I make to share with family and friends. Not to mention simple instructions on how to make the best Chinese classics, from noodles to rice, dumplings and more. There are plenty of tips on making dishes vegetarian, substituting ingredients, and even some healthy air-frying alternatives to deep-frying.

My recipes focus on Hong Kong and Shanghainese cuisines, as these are the cities I grew up in. Hong Kong food, in general, is much lighter than Shanghainese. Hong Kongers often steam and season dishes lightly to bring out the natural flavors. Shanghainese cuisine, on the other hand, is richer and sweeter. Dishes are often stewed or braised, and seasoned with dark soy sauce, which gives them a beautiful dark brown color. You are bound to find a recipe here that satisfies your latest food craving, whatever it is.

Food has always been the center of my life. My grandparents ran a grocery store and a restaurant in Hong Kong. My grandmother, the matriarch of the family, is the best cook I know and whips up some of the most amazing feasts from a kitchen the size of an elevator. My father learned how to cook from her, and I inherited my love of cooking from both of them. (My mother, bless her, is a terrible cook, but was always there to critique my father's cooking!)

I've always turned to food to feel connected to my Chinese heritage. I was born in Sydney, Australia, and my family moved to Hong Kong soon after I was born. We then moved to Shanghai, where we lived for many years. I went on to spend a good deal of time living in the US and the UK, for university and the early years of my career in the food industry. It was during my time in London, when I was feeling the most homesick, that I decided to re-learn the recipes I remembered from my childhood. I started to record and share cooking videos online and (accidentally) became a food content creator!

More than a collection of recipes, this book is a diary of my food memories growing up in China. The scallion pancakes (page 180) remind me of biking along the streets of Shanghai, guided by the smell of scallions frying in hot oil. Steamed white-cut chicken (page 102) takes me right back to my grandparents' house in Kowloon, surrounded by my large extended family. These are my most cherished food memories that I can't wait for you to experience in your own home kitchens as you cook your way through this book.

Key to abbreviations

VE — Vegan
VG — Vegetarian
PESC — Pescatarian

basic pantry ingredients

I firmly believe that Chinese cuisine is one of the easiest cuisines to cook at home. It's essentially the same seasonings over and over again, added in varying quantities and at different stages of a recipe. Once you have a well-stocked Chinese pantry, you can cook everything in this book and more besides. All the ingredients that follow are readily available at big supermarkets.

Note
Where I specify neutral cooking oil for recipes, you can use any neutral-tasting oil of your choice, such as canola, vegetable, corn, peanut or sunflower oil, etc. For deep frying, I like to use oils with a high smoke-point, like canola.

1. Light soy sauce, *sheng chou* 生抽

Light soy sauce is the most frequently used ingredient in Chinese cuisine. It acts like salt to season dishes, and is often used with sugar or dark soy sauce to balance its saltiness. The first character in the Chinese name refers to how it is "young"—less aged than dark soy sauce. When cooking with light soy sauce, I tend to add it towards the end of the cooking time to prevent the dish from getting too salty, which can happen if it is added at the beginning.

2. Dark soy sauce, *lao chou* 老抽

Dark soy sauce is darker in color and has a higher sugar content than light soy sauce. With a molasses-like consistency, it is used to add sweetness and a golden brown color to dishes. The first character in the Chinese name refers to it as "old"—so more aged than light soy sauce. Prominently used in Shanghainese cuisine, dark soy is great at balancing out the saltiness of light soy sauce. Because the seasoning is quite rich, use sparingly.

3. Sesame oil, *ma you* 麻油

Sesame oil is made from toasted sesame seeds and has a strong nutty aroma. It's used sparingly because it can easily overpower a dish with its distinct flavor. It has a low smoke point, which makes it unsuitable for high-heat wok frying or deep-frying. Depending on where it's produced (i.e. Japan, Korea or China), sesame oils vary in flavor. I use sesame oil from Chinese brands to make my dishes taste more authentic.

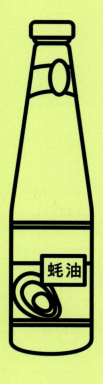

4. Oyster sauce/ Mushroom stir-fry sauce, *hao you* 蚝油

Traditionally, oyster sauce was made by cooking fresh oysters for hours until a thick, dark-brown syrup was obtained. Nowadays, oyster sauce is often made by combining oyster extract with sugar and cornstarch. Oyster sauce is salty and adds a savory depth of flavor to dishes. A wonderful vegetarian alternative is mushroom stir-fry sauce, which is made from mushroom extract. Since oyster/ mushroom stir-fry sauce is very salty, I use it cautiously in my cooking.

5. Shaoxing rice wine, *shao xing jiu* 绍兴酒

Shaoxing wine is the cooking wine I use in this book because it is widely available. However, there are many types of cooking wine in China. Made from fermented glutinous rice, the brownish clear liquid adds a rich depth of flavor to dishes—very similar to adding sherry or red wine in Western cooking. It's an ingredient I highly recommend for home cooks who want to elevate their Chinese cooking. If you're unable to find Shaoxing wine, other clear cooking wines will work.

6. Cornstarch, *yu mi dian fen* 玉米淀粉

Cornstarch is a fine flour made from corn grains and is widely used in Chinese cuisine to thicken soups, stir-fries or to marinate meat. To thicken sauces, we add a "cornstarch slurry," or a mixture of cornstarch and cold water. Cornstarch activates when boiled, so I always add it on low heat to prevent it from immediately curdling when added to a boiling liquid. Once brought back to a boil, the cornstarch reacts and immediately thickens into a silky glaze. Instead of cornstarch, you can also use potato or tapioca starch.

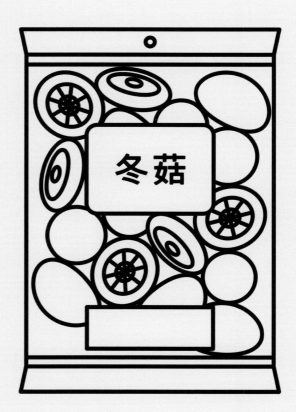

7. Ground white pepper, *hu jiao fen* 胡椒粉

In Chinese cooking, ground white pepper is used in place of black pepper. Black pepper is made from cooked dried unripe peppercorns, while white pepper is made from the peppercorn picked at full ripeness. The flavor is milder and more delicate than black pepper. However, when used in large amounts it can be quite spicy (like in a hot and sour soup). You can buy pre-ground white pepper, which is what I use, or buy whole white peppercorns that you can place in a pepper grinder.

8. Dried mushrooms, *dong gu* 冬菇

Dried shiitake mushrooms are an essential ingredient in Chinese cooking and are used to add a depth of flavor. The mushrooms are dried at a low temperature, which concentrates their flavor, making them very different in flavor and texture to fresh mushrooms. To rehydrate dried shiitake mushrooms, place them in a bowl covered with cold water and leave to soak for at least 4 hours, or up to overnight for best results. I often soak a large batch in an airtight container and leave it in the fridge to use throughout the week. If you're in a hurry, you can also place them in a pot with water and boil for 10–15 minutes, until fully hydrated.

Another popular dried mushroom is woodear, which is actually a fungus. With a unique jelly-like texture, woodear is often used in cold dishes or stir fries. To rehydrate woodear mushrooms, place them in a bowl of cold water and leave to soak for 10 minutes, until soft.

specialty ingredients

The list that follows includes ingredients that might require a visit to an Asian supermarket, but are worth the trip. These are ingredients you can't find in most large supermarkets. None of them are expensive or hard to find. I highly recommend picking up some of these items to make your Chinese dishes taste more authentic.

1. chile bean paste, *dou ban jiang* 豆瓣酱

This salty, spicy condiment is made from fermented broad beans, chiles and soybeans. Also called broad bean paste, it is prominently used in Sichuanese cuisine, but also in other regions in China. Depending on the brand, the flavor of the chile bean paste can vary greatly. Some chile bean pastes in Sichuan are very, very spicy! However, the varieties sold in large supermarkets are milder and only pack heat when used in large amounts.

2. Black rice vinegar, *xiang cu* 香醋

Sometimes called Chinkiang or Zhenjiang vinegar, this is one of my favorite types of vinegar. Made from black glutinous rice, it has a distinct smoky, tart flavor and almost black color. Widely used throughout mainland China, it's delicious when added to a sauce or simply used for dipping. I highly recommend it because of its unique flavor. However, you can also substitute balsamic vinegar or other light-colored vinegars.

3. Chinese sesame paste, *zhi ma jiang* 芝麻酱

Similar to tahini, Chinese sesame paste is a thick paste made from blended sesame seeds. However, its made from toasted sesame seeds so it has a distinctly nuttier flavor and a darker color. It adds a rich creaminess and earthiness to dishes such as cold appetizers, salads or noodles. If you can't find Chinese sesame paste, you can use tahini or unsweetened peanut butter, but the final result will taste a bit different.

4. Chinese sausage, *lap cheong* 腊肠

This is a preserved pork sausage with varying ratios of meat to fat, often added to stir-fries or rice dishes to add a smoky, salty flavor. Growing up, my grandma often had Chinese sausages hanging by a string on her windowsill to continue drying and curing. We sometimes throw it into the rice cooker so it steams as the rice cooks and infuses the rice with more flavor. Due to its unique flavor, there isn't a great substitute, but if you can't find it you can simply omit from the recipe.

5. Varieties of tofu, dou fu 豆腐

In Hong Kong, you'll find stalls in wet markets (fresh food markets) that only sell soybean products—dozens of them, from sheets of dried tofu skin, pressed and marinated tofu, to deep-fried tofu puffs. In the West, most tofu is packaged in liquid to help it stay moist and fresh. To store leftover tofu, place it in an airtight container and cover with cold water. Store in the fridge for up to 3–4 days.

a. Silken tofu: A soft, jelly-like tofu made from coagulated soy milk, this crumbles easily and must be handled with care. We often add silken tofu to soups or stews with vegetables, seafood and meat.

b. Medium-firm tofu: This is the type of tofu sold in most grocery stores. It is more compact than silken tofu and doesn't crumble as easily. It has a wide variety of cooking applications—it can be pan-fried, crumbled, or added to soups and stews.

c. Firm tofu: This variety of tofu is harder and drier, and more suitable for pan-frying or crumbling. When squeezed, some liquid should wring out—it shouldn't be completely dry. I find that some firm tofu products sold in the West are much firmer and drier than firm tofu in Asia.

6. Varieties of noodles, mian 面

Similar to tofu shops, there are noodle shops in Hong Kong that only sell fresh hand-made noodles of varying thicknesses, lengths and textures. Some are made for stir-frying, some to be served in soups, and others for deep-frying into a crisp. Below, I outline just a few of the noodle varieties that are most commonly found in the West.

a. Rice noodles: These noodles are made with rice flour and, depending on the brand's ratio of rice flour to water, the texture of the noodle can vary. Sometimes sold fresh or dried into sticks of varying thicknesses and shapes, these noodles can be used in soups or stir-fries. To cook dried rice noodles, place into a large bowl and cover with warm water. Leave to soak for 10–15 minutes until just tender. You don't want to over-soak the noodles, otherwise they'll be too soft when stir-fried or served in a soup.

b. Wheat noodles: Here, I'm generally referring to noodles made with wheat flour, sometimes with added egg or lye water to change the texture and color of the noodles. In Hong Kong, many of the wheat noodles are treated with lye water to give them a slightly chewier texture and/or yellow color. Most wheat noodles need to be boiled in a large pan of water, but depending on size and shape cooking times can vary greatly. Always refer to the package instructions or taste the noodles to check for doneness.

c. Alternative flour noodles: Apart from rice-flour and wheat-flour noodles, there are also a large variety of noodles made with alternative flours: brown rice noodles, green bean (or mung bean) noodles, sweet potato noodles, and so on. Next time you're in the noodle aisle at an Asian supermarket, I urge you to try out different types of noodles. These are great options for people who are gluten-free. Many of these noodles cook quicker and more evenly when soaked in cold water for 10 minutes to soften before boiling.

7. Varieties of rice, *fan* 饭

China is one of the largest growers and exporters of rice in the world. It is an essential part of any meal. Growing up, we had a freshly cooked pot of rice with every dinner. The Chinese slang for someone who can eat a lot is *fan tong* 饭桶, which means "rice bucket." But it also means someone who only loves to eat and doesn't do much else!

<u>a. Jasmine rice:</u> This is the variety of rice that most Chinese families enjoy at home. It's a type of long-grain rice that is slightly shorter than Indian Basmati rice. It tastes delicate and fragrant, and can be steamed, used in fried rice or cooked into congee (a savory Chinese rice porridge).

<u>b. Sushi rice:</u> Sometimes called sticky rice, this is a short-grain rice most commonly eaten in Japan. The grain is short, stubby and higher in starch than long-grain rice. It also tastes slightly creamier and richer. Some Hong Kong families eat sushi rice at home because they prefer the sweet flavor.

<u>c. Sticky glutinous rice:</u> Also sometimes called sticky rice, this rice variety tastes richer and chewier than short- and long-grain rice. Glutinous rice is high in starch and opaque when raw, but once cooked turns sticky and slightly translucent. It is sometimes wrapped in lotus leaves and steamed with chicken for dim sum, or cooked with coconut milk and turned into desserts.

how to cook perfect rice

Time
18–20 minutes

Ingredients
1¼ cups (240 g) jasmine rice (a heaped ¼ cup/ 60 g uncooked rice per person)

1 cup (240 ml) cold water

Serves 4 as a side

Here are three methods of cooking rice, from the easiest and most foolproof to cooking in a rice cooker. I always wash all varieties of rice under running cold water first, to remove dirt and excess starch. I also sometimes soak the rice to speed up the cooking time. I like to use the same measuring tool every time I cook rice. For example, if I fill my favorite coffee mug with rice and it cooks a perfect amount of rice for 3 people, then I know to cook 2 coffee mugs of rice if I ever need to cook for 6 people.

As a general rule, the ratio of uncooked to cooked rice is 1:3. So, ½ cup (100 g) dry rice will make around 1½ cups (300 g) cooked rice. For a single portion of rice as a side, I recommend around ¼ cup (50–60 g) dry rice. For a single portion of rice as a main, I recommend around ½ cup (100–120 g) dry rice. For a fried rice dish, I recommend using slightly less rice, as the dish becomes larger from the added protein and veggies. So, to make fried rice for a hungry family of four as a main, you'll want at least 1¾ cups (350 g) dry rice, or around 5¼ cups (1 kg) cooked.

Measuring

First, measure the amount of rice you want to cook with a mug or measuring cup. Place into a large bowl and rinse under running cold water until the water is almost clear, around 1–2 minutes (see Note, opposite, for cooking Japanese sushi rice). Drain well.

Boiling method

I use this method to cook all types of grains, like quinoa, brown rice, barley, etc. Bring a large pot (with a tight-fitting lid) of water to a boil (no need to measure it). Add the rinsed rice and boil for 12–14 minutes until cooked through. Drain in a sieve or fine colander, then return the rice to the pot. Cover with the lid and leave the rice to stand for at least 5 minutes, with the heat off. The leftover heat in the pot will evaporate any excess water and make the rice fluffier. Remove the lid and fluff the rice with a rubber or rice spatula.

Evaporation method

Place the measured, rinsed rice into a medium saucepan with a tight-fitting lid. Measure the equal amount of cold water and add it to the pan. Cover with the lid and bring to a boil (do not open the lid again until the very end of cooking). The moment the water boils, immediately turn the heat to low and simmer for 12–14 minutes. Turn the heat off and leave the rice to stand for at least 5 minutes, with the lid on. This allows excess water to evaporate. Remove the lid and fluff the rice with a rubber or rice spatula.

Rice cooker method

Place the measured, rinsed rice into the rice cooker pot. Measure the equal amount of cold water and add it to the pot. Close the lid and turn the rice cooker on (see Note). Once the rice is cooked, leave to stand in the rice cooker for at least 5 minutes for any excess water to evaporate. Open the lid and fluff the rice with a rubber or rice spatula.

Cooling rice

If using freshly cooked rice in fried rice, transfer the cooked rice to 1–2 large trays or plates and gently spread into a thin layer with a rubber or rice spatula, being careful not to break up the rice grains. Leave to steam-dry and cool completely before using in a fried rice recipe. If you add steaming-hot, freshly cooked rice to a wok, it most often results in soggy fried rice. Typically, I use leftover rice from the day before that has been stored in an airtight container in the fridge and break up any large clumps before adding it to the wok.

Notes

If using Japanese sushi rice, wash for longer—the grains are higher in starch and will stick to each other if not rinsed properly.

Some rice cookers simply have an "on" and "off" button, while others offer multiple rice-cooking functions. I usually use the most basic rice-cooking function.

how to steam things

One of the most popular cooking methods in Chinese cuisine is steaming, where food is cooked by the heat of evaporating boiling water. It's a healthy and easy way to prepare a dish, since it doesn't require any additional oil or much active cooking. Electric steamers and steamer pans are available, but typically, in China, a wok is filled with a small amount of boiling water, then a bamboo steamer basket with a lid is placed into the wok (without letting it directly touch the water). The basket can then be filled with whatever you want to steam. Steamer baskets are great, because they allow you to place an entire dish of food into the basket, which will retain all the delicious cooking juices released during steaming. You can also line steamer baskets with parchment paper to steam buns, dumplings and/or vegetables.

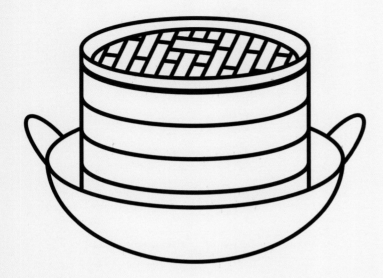

If you don't have a steamer basket, there are many other methods you can use to steam cook using items you may already have in your kitchen:

- Roll up pieces of aluminum foil into small balls, then place them into a deep pot. Fill the pot with boiling water, halfway or two-thirds up the height of the foil balls, then place your dish directly on top of the foil. Cover with a lid and steam your dish over medium or medium-high heat, keeping the water simmering or boiling.

- Instead of foil, place a heatproof bowl (ceramic or stainless steel) in the base of the pot, then place the dish on top of this.

- In Asia, kitchen supply stores often sell small metal racks that allow you to place larger dishes (that don't fit into a steamer basket) into a pot to steam. Alternatively, metal steamer baskets are widely available and are great for steaming vegetables and some proteins, but less useful for steaming whole dishes.

chinese dining etiquette

Here's a brief list of the dos and don'ts when dining at a Chinese restaurant, either for dinner or dim sum in the afternoon.

In a typical dim sum restaurant, printed paper menus and pencils are placed on the table. You're expected to check what you'd like to order, then hand the menu to the waiter.

At the beginning of the meal, as well as tea, you're given a large kettle of hot water and a large, empty bowl. These are for cleaning and sanitizing your dishes and utensils before the meal. It's a cultural habit that dates back to when Hong Kong was a poor city and people were worried about hygiene. It's not compulsory.

A dim sim menu is usually divided into different sections, such as appetizers, steamed dishes, mains like rice or noodles, and sides like vegetables. One of the special features of dim sum is that you eat savory and sweet dishes at the same time. It's very normal to enjoy a sweet egg tart, then take a bite of steamed shrimp dumpling right after. Everything is served in either three or four pieces, so you have to order a large variety of dishes to feed the whole table.

It's common practice that the younger members of the group pour tea for everyone else at the table and continue to top up teacups throughout the meal. To thank someone who has refilled your cup of tea, tap the tip of your index and middle finger twice onto the table right next to the teacup. This represents a traditional kowtow (a full bow), which was performed in tea ceremonies to express gratitude. If the teapot needs to be refilled with hot water, leave the lid slightly ajar and this signifies to the staff that your table needs more tea.

Many Chinese restaurants have lazy Susans (turntables), because in Chinese culture all dishes are meant to be shared. It would be considered very rude to order a dish just for yourself. If you're eating around a lazy Susan, never move it when someone else is already moving it. Wait for someone to finish serving themselves before turning the lazy Susan in your direction.

You are usually given two pairs of chopsticks in different colors— one for picking up food from the shared dishes, and one for eating from your own bowl. This keeps communal dining more hygienic. Today, many dishes also come with serving spoons for ease.

When eating with chopsticks, you should never leave them stuck pointing down into the middle of a dish. This resembles the burning of incense at a funeral or the stabbing of the heart and is considered very rude.

At the end of a Chinese meal, it's common for one bite of food to be left on every plate. That's because the last bite of food should always be offered to others first. It is also considered rude to leave uneaten food in your bowl (this is why my British partner always ends up overeating at my Chinese family meals). If there are remaining bits of food left in your bowl, bring the bowl closer to your mouth to scoop up the last bites. Many parents tell their children different folktales to get them to finish their bowl of rice. My parents used to tell me that if I didn't finish the last grain of rice then my future partner would be unattractive! Of course, I ate every last grain!

Last but not least, another unwritten Chinese custom is to play tug of war for the bill. Splitting the bill is not common in Chinese culture and the host will usually offer to pay it. This most often means that by the time someone has offered to pay, someone else has already sneakily gone to take care of it.

chapter

whip up on a weeknight

one

葱油拌面
Scallion Oil Noodles VE

Time
18–20 minutes

Ingredients

5 tbsp neutral cooking oil

6 scallions, cut into 2 in (5 cm) pieces, then julienned

2 servings (7 oz (200 g) thin wheat noodles

1 tbsp dark soy sauce

2 tsp light soy sauce

½ tsp sugar

½ tsp salt

When I think of Shanghainese cuisine, this is the first dish that comes to mind, with its beautiful amber sauce and the aroma of frying scallions that you can smell from the other side of the kitchen. You don't want to rush the frying of the scallions, otherwise they might burn. Instead, fry them low and slow to infuse the oil with plenty of scallion flavor.

Combine the oil and most of the scallions (save some for garnish) in a small saucepan over medium-low heat. Cook for 13–15 minutes, stirring occasionally, until golden brown. Reduce the heat if the scallions brown too quickly.

Halfway through cooking the scallions, cook the noodles in a separate pot according to the package instructions. Drain, then transfer to serving bowls.

Remove the scallions from the heat and mix in the dark soy sauce, light soy sauce, sugar and salt. Taste to adjust the seasonings.

Divide the sauce evenly between the noodles, garnish with the reserved scallions and serve.

Serves 4

葱油猪扒饭
Pork Chop with Scallion Sauce and Rice

Time

25–30 minutes, plus 20 minutes or overnight marinating

Ingredients

4 boneless pork chops

2 tbsp neutral cooking oil, plus 2 tsp

4 eggs

salt and ground white pepper, to taste

4 servings of cooked jasmine rice (see pages 18–19)

4 tbsp Sweet Soy Sauce (see page 191) (or regular light soy sauce)

For the marinade

⅓ cup (80 ml) water

1 tbsp light soy sauce

2 tsp cornstarch

1 tsp salt

1 tsp sugar

½ tsp baking soda (see Note)

pinch of ground white pepper

For the scallion sauce

4 tbsp neutral cooking oil

6 scallions, sliced into ½ in (1 cm) pieces (white and green parts separated)

½ tsp salt

½ tsp sugar

If you walk into a *cha chaan teng* 茶餐廳, or Cantonese-style diner during lunch hour, you'll probably see someone eating this dish. Think crispy marinated pork chops seared on a flat-top grill, served with freshly steamed rice, a fried egg, a drizzle of soy and a glorious scallion sauce. The only thing missing is a refreshing glass of iced lemon tea on the side.

Place the pork chops on a chopping board. Using the back edge of a knife or a meat tenderizer, bash the chops into cutlets, about ½ in (1.5 cm) thick. Cut small indents into the curved edge of each chop, so they remain flat while frying. Place in a bowl and add the marinade ingredients. Gently massage for 2–3 minutes. Leave to marinate for at least 20 minutes, or overnight in the fridge for best results.

For the scallion sauce, heat a medium frying pan over medium-low heat. Add the oil and scallion whites, and cook for 6–8 minutes until lightly golden brown.

Place the scallion greens, salt and sugar in a small bowl and mix, then add the hot scallion oil and mix. Taste to adjust the seasoning.

Heat the 2 tablespoons of cooking oil in a wok or frying pan over medium heat. In batches, add the pork chops and cook for 4–5 minutes on each side until golden and cooked through. Transfer to a plate and leave to rest.

Add the 2 teaspoons of oil to the same pan and reheat over medium heat. Crack in the eggs and fry for 3–5 minutes, or until the whites have set and the yolks are runny. Season with salt and white pepper.

Serve the pork chops on a plate alongside the rice topped with a fried egg, drizzled with sweet soy sauce (or regular light soy sauce). Serve the scallion sauce on the side.

Note

Chinese chefs and home cooks often use baking soda to tenderize meat. This process is called "velveting." Some people only add baking soda, while others also add egg white, cornstarch and oil to get silky, tender meat. You only need a small amount of baking soda to achieve velvet-tender meat—too much will affect the flavor.

Serves 2

电饭煲炖饭

Easy Rice Cooker Dinner VE OPTION

Time
25–30 minutes

Ingredients
⅔ cup (140 g) jasmine rice

2 tsp neutral cooking oil

1 Chinese sausage, diced (optional)

¼ cabbage, roughly diced

1 carrot, roughly diced

generous ½ cup (140 ml) water

1 scallion, thinly sliced, to garnish

For the sauce
2 tsp dark soy sauce

1 tsp light soy sauce

1 tsp oyster sauce (or mushroom stir-fry sauce)

2 tsp sesame oil

pinch of ground white pepper

This easy rice cooker dinner has saved me on nights when I couldn't be bothered to cook. Chop your ingredients, pop everything into the rice cooker, then wait for it to sing you a little tune to tell you it's ready. If you don't have a rice cooker, you can easily prepare this dish in a pot with a tight-fitting lid. You can use any vegetables, just make sure to chop everything into roughly the same size so it cooks evenly. For a vegan version, omit the Chinese sausage and swap in mushroom stir-fry sauce for the oyster sauce.

Rinse the rice under running cold water until the water is almost clear, 1–2 minutes. Drain well, then place in the rice cooker (or a pot with a tight-fitting lid—see Note) and set aside.

Transfer the vegetable mixture to the rice cooker. Add the ingredients for the sauce directly into the rice cooker. Add the measured water (or equal volume of water to the weight of rice) and mix to combine. Cook according to the machine instructions (or see Note).

Taste to adjust the seasoning. Serve in bowls, garnished with the sliced scallion.

Note
For stovetop cooking, place the uncooked rice, vegetables, sauce and measured water into a pot. Mix to combine and cover with a tight-fitting lid. Bring to a boil, then reduce the heat to low and simmer for 13–15 minutes until the rice is cooked. Once the rice is cooked, turn off the heat. Leave the rice to stand for 5 minutes with the lid on. Remove the lid and fluff the rice with a rubber or rice spatula.

玉米鸡汤

Chicken and Corn Soup

This is one of my mom's favorite soups that my dad makes. My dad's secret is frying off the chicken in a little bit of butter to bring out its flavors, then adding a small splash of milk to make the soup creamier. The mixture of creamed corn and regular corn also gives the soup a wonderful texture. My dad always makes this soup when he has leftover chicken in the fridge.

Time
20 minutes

Ingredients
1 tbsp butter

5¼ oz (150 g) skinless chicken breast or thigh, thinly sliced into strips (or leftover shredded cooked chicken)

1¾ cups (300 g) canned corn kernels

14 oz (400 g) can cream-style corn

1¼ cups (300 ml) water or chicken stock

3–4 tbsp milk

2 eggs

1 tbsp water

2 scallions, thinly sliced, to garnish

salt and ground white pepper

For the cornstarch slurry
1 tbsp cornstarch

3½ tbsp water

Heat a large pot over medium heat. Add the butter and cook for 1–2 minutes to melt, then add the chicken and cook for 2–3 minutes until very lightly golden. Season with salt and white pepper. Add the corn, cream-style corn, water or chicken stock and milk to the pot, bring to a boil, then reduce the heat to low and simmer for 5–10 minutes.

Meanwhile, in a small bowl, beat the eggs with a tablespoon of water until smooth. Season with salt and white pepper.

In a separate small bowl, make the cornstarch slurry by mixing together the cornstarch and water.

Slowly add the cornstarch slurry to the soup, while continuously stirring. Bring to a boil for 2–3 minutes until thickened. Reduce the heat back to low, then slowly pour in the eggs, while continuously stirring. Taste to adjust the seasoning.

Divide among serving bowls and garnish with the scallions.

Serves 2

上海粗炒
Shanghai Stir-Fried Thick Noodles VE

Time
15 minutes

Ingredients

2 servings of udon noodles (or thick wheat noodles) (see Note)

2 tsp neutral cooking oil

9 oz (250 g) bok choi or cabbage (or any other leafy green), thinly sliced

2 scallions, cut into thirds

4 dried shiitake mushrooms, rehydrated and thinly sliced

For the sauce

1 tbsp black rice vinegar

1 tbsp dark soy sauce

2 tsp light soy sauce

1 tsp sesame oil

½ tsp sugar

½ tsp salt

The dish is one of Shanghai's most famous noodle dishes. What makes this dish special is the type of noodles used—a very thick-cut wheat noodle. I like to use frozen Japanese udon because I think it's most similar to the type of noodles they use in Shanghai. The noodles are also coated in a sauce before stir-frying, which is not typical of Chinese noodle stir-fries, making this one of the easiest noodle dishes in this book.

If necessary, cook the udon noodles according to the package instructions. Drain, then transfer to a large bowl. Add the ingredients for the sauce and toss well to combine. Set aside.

Heat the oil in a large wok or frying pan over high heat. Add the bok choi and scallions, and cook for 3–4 minutes until softening. Add the mushrooms and the noodles in their sauce, and cook for 2–3 minutes, tossing to combine. Taste to adjust the seasonings.

Transfer to a large plate and serve immediately.

Note

I personally think the texture and flavor of frozen udon is much better than packaged, cooked udon. However, if you're using pre-cooked udon (sometimes labeled "quick to cook" or "straight to wok" udon) there is no need to boil/cook the udon. You can simply place in a bowl and mix with the sauce, then stir-fry as the recipe instructs.

Serves 2

茄汁虾碌
Ketchup Shrimp ^{PESC}

Time
15–20 minutes

Ingredients
2 tsp neutral cooking oil

2 shallots (or 1 small red onion), thinly sliced

small piece of fresh ginger root, peeled and sliced into thin discs

2 scallions, cut into thirds

2 garlic cloves, roughly chopped

2 small tomatoes, roughly chopped

2 tbsp ketchup

1 tbsp Shaoxing rice wine

6½ oz (180 g) raw shrimp (shell-on or off), deveined

dash of Worcestershire sauce

1 tsp light soy sauce

1 tsp dark soy sauce

½ tsp sugar

½ tsp salt

pinch of ground white pepper

small handful of fresh cilantro, roughly torn, to garnish

Since Hong Kong was a former British colony, there are many Western ingredients that have been completely woven into the Chinese pantry. My grandmother always has ketchup, Worcestershire sauce and even British baked beans in her pantry. Chinese chefs love adding a small amount of ketchup to add sweetness, acidity and to thicken sauces.

Heat the oil in a large wok or frying pan over high heat. Add the shallots and cook for 1–2 minutes until softening. Add the ginger, scallions and garlic, and cook for 2–3 minutes until fragrant. Add the tomatoes and ketchup and stir to combine. Once bubbling, pour the rice wine around the edges of the pan, then add the shrimp and cook for 6–8 minutes until cooked through. (If using shell-on shrimp, cook for an additional 2–3 minutes.) Add all the remaining ingredients and stir to combine. Taste to adjust the seasonings.

Transfer to a plate and serve garnished with the cilantro.

Note

A theory behind the history of ketchup is that the English word derives from the Cantonese word *keh jup* 茄汁, which refers to a pickled fish brine. In fact, ketchup was originally more of a fish sauce and did not turn into a tomato-based condiment until Heinz added tomatoes in the 1800s to help prolong shelf life.

whip up on a weeknight

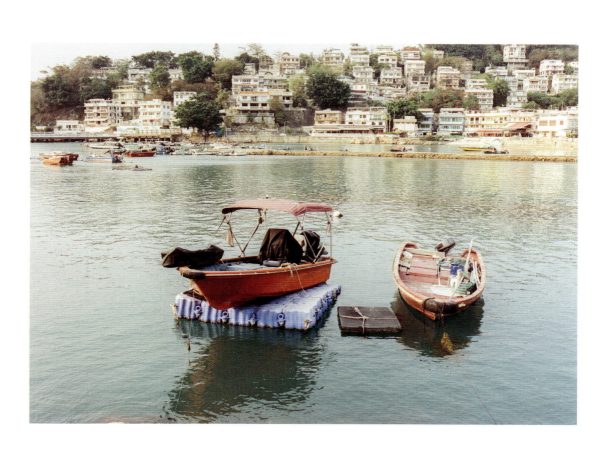

Serves 2

番茄炒蛋

Tomato and Egg Stir-Fry VG

Time
15–19 minutes

Ingredients
1 tsp neutral cooking oil

3 medium tomatoes, cut into thin wedges

3 scallions, sliced into thirds

1 tbsp mushroom stir-fry sauce

1 tbsp ketchup

2 tbsp water

½ tsp salt

pinch of ground white pepper

For the eggs
2 tsp neutral cooking oil

4 eggs, beaten

salt and ground white pepper, to taste

For the cornstarch slurry
2 tsp cornstarch

2 tbsp water

This is what I make on busy weeknights when I need food fast. All Chinese families have their own recipe for this—some with delicate bits of scrambled eggs, some with well-cooked chunks. How you like your eggs scrambled is up to you. My version creates a thick and luscious sauce that coats the scrambled eggs. Perfect for enjoying with some rice or noodles, or served alongside a larger meal. *Pictured overleaf.*

Start with the eggs. Heat the oil in a wok or frying pan over high heat. Pour in the eggs and cook for 2–3 minutes, then run the spatula across the width of the pan and scramble until there are large and small chunks of scrambled eggs. Season with salt and white pepper. Transfer to a bowl and set aside.

Add the teaspoon of oil to the same pan, then add the tomatoes and most of the scallions (reserve a little and finely slice for garnish), and cook for 2–3 minutes until softened. Add the mushroom stir-fry sauce, ketchup, water, salt and white pepper. Cook for 3–4 minutes until a sauce forms.

In a separate small bowl, make the cornstarch slurry by mixing together the cornstarch and water.

Reduce the heat to medium and slowly add the cornstarch slurry to the pan, while continuously stirring. Cook for 2–3 minutes until the sauce thickens. Return the scrambled eggs to the pan and mix. Taste to adjust the seasoning.

Transfer to a plate and garnish with the reserved sliced scallions. Serve on its own or with a bowl of freshly cooked rice or noodles.

Serves 2

豉汁豆腐
Black Bean Tofu VE

This is a classic pairing in Chinese cuisine. Combining salty, fermented black beans (which are in fact soybeans) with another soybean product—tofu. There are so many different ways to prepare this combo: steamed, pan-fried, stuffed or stewed. In my version, crispy pan-fried tofu gets tossed with crunchy vegetables and a delicious black bean sauce. I've used different colored peppers here, but use whatever vegetables you have on hand. *Pictured overleaf.*

Time
20–25 minutes

Ingredients
2 tsp neutral cooking oil

½ red bell pepper, cut into ¾ in (2 cm) chunks

½ green bell pepper, cut into ¾ in (2 cm) chunks

½ white onion, cut into ¾ in (2 cm) chunks

2 garlic cloves, finely chopped

1 small piece of fresh ginger root, peeled and finely chopped

½ cup (120 ml) water

For the tofu
2 tsp neutral cooking oil

1 x 14 oz (400 g) block of medium-firm tofu, halved lengthways, then cut into ½ in (1 cm) thick rectangles

salt, to taste

For the sauce
1 tbsp fermented black beans, rinsed

2 tbsp Shaoxing rice wine

4 tsp mushroom stir-fry sauce

4 tsp light soy sauce

1 tsp dark soy sauce

2 tsp sesame oil

1 tsp sugar

For the cornstarch slurry
2 tsp cornstarch

2 tbsp water

Start with the tofu. Heat the oil in a nonstick frying pan over medium heat. Add the tofu and cook for 6–8 minutes, turning halfway through, until golden brown. Season with salt. Transfer to a plate and set aside.

In a small bowl, mix together the ingredients for the sauce.

In a separate small bowl, mix together the ingredients for the cornstarch slurry.

Heat the oil in a large wok or pan over high heat. Add the pepper and onion, and cook for 3–4 minutes until lightly charred. Add the garlic and ginger, and cook for 1–2 minutes until fragrant. Add the sauce around the edges of the pan and cook for 1–2 minutes until sizzling. Add the pan-fried tofu and water, and gently stir to combine. Cook for 3–4 minutes until slightly reduced.

Reduce the heat to low and slowly pour in the cornstarch slurry while continuously mixing. Cook for 1–2 minutes until the sauce thickens. Taste to adjust the seasonings.

Transfer to a plate and serve.

Note
Fermented black beans are a common ingredient in Cantonese kitchens. Made from cooked, brined, then dried soybeans, they are used as a salt to season dishes. Since they are so salty, they often need to be soaked in cold water, then drained before use. Black bean stir-fry sauces, a popular ingredient sold in many grocery stores worldwide, derive from fermented black beans.

Serves 2

香菇蒸鸡
Steamed Chicken and Mushrooms

Time
30 minutes

Ingredients
10½ oz (300 g) boneless chicken thighs (skin-on or off), cut into ¾ in (2 cm) pieces

4 dried shiitake mushrooms, rehydrated

1 large piece of fresh ginger root, peeled and sliced into thin discs

For the marinade
1 tbsp Shaoxing rice wine

2 tsp light soy sauce

2 tsp oyster sauce

1 tsp sesame oil

½ tsp sugar

1 tsp cornstarch

Steaming is one of the most popular methods of cooking in Cantonese cuisine, and steamed chicken with mushrooms is one of the most classic home-cooked dishes. In this recipe, chicken is marinated, then infused with shiitake mushrooms and ginger, creating a delicious sauce that I could drink straight from the bowl. I always enjoy this dish with a fresh bowl of rice to mop up all the drinkable sauce.

Place the chicken in a large bowl, add all the ingredients for the marinade and mix to combine. Leave to marinate while you prepare the rest of the ingredients, or overnight in the fridge.

Prepare a steamer large enough to hold the chicken (see pages 20–1).

Place the mushrooms and ginger into a large, shallow, heatproof dish. Place the chicken on top of the vegetables. Pour over any remaining marinade. Wrap tightly in plastic wrap (this will help the chicken cook quicker).

Place the dish in the steamer and steam over medium-high heat for 18–20 minutes until the chicken is cooked through. Serve with a side of rice to soak up all the sauce.

Note
The amount of time it takes to steam your chicken depends on the depth of the steaming dish. I advise using a shallow plate, because the chicken will cook quicker. Feel free to add thinly sliced Chinese sausage for a smoky flavor, or greens such as broccoli or bok choi, or substitute with fresh mushrooms like button or cremini. Add these ingredients at the same time as the chicken.

Serves 2

蒸水蛋
Steamed Egg ^{VG}

Time
20 minutes

Ingredients
2 eggs
around scant ½ cup (100 ml) water or stock (any kind)
½ tsp salt
pinch of ground white pepper

To garnish
1 scallion, thinly sliced
2 tsp light soy sauce (optional)

This dish was on a weekly rotation growing up—simple steamed eggs with a beautiful custard-like texture. There are so many variations—sometimes my dad adds dried seafood or even ground pork on top. My trick for getting the perfect ratio of egg to water is using a clear measuring cup or glass. That way, it's easy to add an equal volume of water to the eggs.

Crack the eggs into a clear measuring cup or glass and whisk until little to no egg whites remain. Add the same amount of water or stock as the volume of the eggs and whisk to combine. Season with the salt and white pepper.

Strain the egg mixture through a fine-mesh sieve into a shallow steaming dish. Remove any remaining foam or bubbles with a spoon. (Alternatively, place a lighter or lit match near the bubbles and they will immediately disappear.) Wrap the dish tightly with plastic wrap.

Prepare a steamer large enough to hold the egg dish (see pages 20–1).

Place the egg dish into your steamer. Steam for 10–12 minutes, or until the eggs are set (it should only slightly jiggle). Turn off the heat and leave to stand for 5 minutes with the lid on.

Garnish the steamed eggs with scallion and a small drizzle of light soy sauce (if wished) and serve.

鸡煲仔饭

Chicken Clay Pot Rice

Time

25 minutes, plus
20 minutes soaking

Ingredients

2 servings (⅔ cup/140 g) uncooked jasmine rice

2 chicken thighs, sliced into ½ in (1.5 cm) strips

3 tsp neutral cooking oil

1 Chinese sausage, thinly sliced at an angle

3 dried shiitake mushrooms, rehydrated and thinly sliced

generous ½ cup (140 ml) cold water (or ⅔ cup/160 ml if cooking in a clay pot)

1 tbsp Sweet Soy Sauce (see page 191) (or 2 tsp light soy sauce plus 1 tsp dark soy sauce)

For the marinade

1 tbsp Shaoxing rice wine

1 tsp cornstarch

1 tsp light soy sauce

1 tsp sesame oil

½ tsp ground white pepper

½ tsp sugar

½ tsp salt

Hong Kong is filled with restaurants that specialize in clay pot rice, served with toppings like steamed pork, salted fish, egg and vegetables. Chicken and Chinese sausage clay pot rice is one of the most popular choices. This dish has a reputation for being difficult to make because it is hard to achieve perfectly cooked rice with that famous crispy bottom. Here, I'm showing you an easier version that you can make in a regular pot or rice cooker.

Place the rice in a large bowl and cover with cold water. Leave to soak for 20 minutes, then drain.

Place the chicken in a small bowl and add the ingredients for the marinade. Leave to marinate while you prepare the rest of the ingredients, or overnight in the fridge.

Heat 2 teaspoons of the oil in a pot or clay pot (with a tight-fitting lid) over medium heat. Add the Chinese sausage and cook for 2–3 minutes until some of the fat has rendered. Transfer to a plate and set aside (see Note for rice cooker method).

Add the rice to the pot and cook for 1–2 minutes, mixing to coat the rice with the sausage fat. Spread the rice into an even layer, then place the marinated chicken, Chinese sausage and mushrooms on top. Add the measured water (or equal volume of water to the weight of rice), cover with a lid and bring to a boil, then reduce the heat to low. Simmer for 14–16 minutes until the rice and chicken is cooked through.

Remove the lid and turn the heat up to medium. Add the remaining teaspoon of oil around the edges of the pot and cook for 3–4 minutes until the rice is crispy on the bottom.

Serve drizzled with sweet soy sauce, or a mixture of light and dark soy sauce.

Note

To cook in a rice cooker, transfer the soaked and drained rice to the rice cooker. Place the marinated chicken and Chinese sausage on top, then pour over the measured water. Cook according to the machine instructions. With this method, you skip the instruction to achieve a crispy bottom on the rice, but it's still equally delicious.

Serves 2-4

上海菜饭
Steamed Vegetable and Bacon Rice

A delicious one-pot meal that can come together in just half an hour. The name of this dish literally translates to "Shanghai vegetable rice," and it's really as simple as that. This recipe traditionally calls for Chinese cured ham, *jin hua huo tui* 金华火腿. However, smoked bacon is an excellent substitute and gives the dish a delicious smoky flavor. If you want, you can also place all the ingredients in a rice cooker and let it do the work for you.

Time

30–38 minutes, plus 20 minutes soaking

Ingredients

2 servings (⅔ cup/140 g) uncooked jasmine rice

1 tsp neutral cooking oil (unless cooking in a rice cooker—see Note)

9 oz (250 g) bok choi (or any other leafy green), finely chopped

2 oz (60 g) smoked bacon or lardons, thinly sliced

1 small piece of fresh ginger root, peeled and sliced into thin discs

generous ½ cup (140 ml) water (or ⅔ cup/160 ml if cooking in a clay pot)

2 tsp sesame oil

salt and ground white pepper, to taste

Place the rice in a bowl and cover with water. Leave to soak for 20 minutes, then drain. This will help the rice cook quicker and more evenly.

Heat the cooking oil in a pot (with a tight-fitting lid) over high heat. Add the bok choi and cook for 3–5 minutes, stirring constantly, until softened. Season with salt. Once cooked, transfer to a small plate and set aside (skip this step if cooking in a rice cooker—see Note).

Reheat the pot over medium heat. Add the bacon and cook for 5–7 minutes, or until some of the fat has rendered. Turn the heat up to high, then add the ginger and cook for 2–3 minutes until fragrant and golden brown. Add the drained rice and cook for 1–2 minutes, stirring constantly, until lightly golden.

Add the measured water (see Note for cooking in a rice coooker). Cover with the lid and bring to a boil. Turn the heat to low and simmer for 14–16 minutes, or until the rice is cooked. Once cooked, turn the heat off and leave the rice to stand for 5 minutes with the lid on.

Remove the lid from the pot. Drain any liquid that has been released from the bok choi, then very gently stir the bok choi through the rice with a rubber or rice spatula. Season with salt and pepper, then taste to adjust. Divide among bowls and serve.

Note

To cook in a rice cooker, transfer the bacon, ginger and rice mixture to a rice cooker. Add the raw chopped bok choi and mix to combine. Cook according to the machine instructions. Season with salt and white pepper, then taste to adjust. Divide among bowls and serve.

免治牛肉蛋饭

Hong Kong-Style Beef Gravy with Rice

Time
35–40 minutes

Ingredients
1 tbsp oil

2 eggs

⅓ cup (50 g) garden peas (optional)

2 servings of cooked jasmine rice (see pages 18–19)

salt and ground white pepper, to taste

For the beef gravy
1 tbsp neutral cooking oil

1 white onion, finely diced

1 carrot, finely diced

2 garlic cloves, finely chopped

9 oz (250 g) ground beef

½ tsp salt

½ tsp ground white pepper

2 tbsp tomato paste

3 tbsp ketchup

1 large tomato, roughly chopped

2 bay leaves

1⅔ cups (400 ml) water or stock

2 tsp light soy sauce

2 tsp oyster sauce

During the 1950s, while Hong Kong was a British colony, chefs started creating dishes that were a mash-up of Western and Chinese cooking. This type of cuisine was later coined "Soy Sauce Western Cuisine," *si yau sai chaan* 豉油西餐, and is beloved by Hong Kongers. There are many restaurants famous for serving this type of cuisine, with waiters dressed in a suit and tie and decor that takes you back in time. One of the many famous dishes is this Cantonese-ified beef bolognese with rice.

Start with the gravy. Heat the oil in a medium pot (that has a lid) over medium heat. Add the onion and carrot, and cook for 5–7 minutes until softened. Add the garlic and beef, and cook for 3–5 minutes until golden brown. Season with the salt and white pepper.

Add the tomato paste and cook for 1–2 minutes until fragrant, then add all the remaining gravy ingredients and cover with a lid. Simmer for 15–20 minutes, or until the gravy has reduced.

Heat the oil in a medium frying pan over medium-high heat. Crack in the eggs and fry for 3–5 minutes, or until the whites have set and the yolks are runny. Season with salt and white pepper.

Taste the beef gravy to adjust the seasoning and stir in the peas (if using) to briefly wilt.

Serve the rice on a plate with a generous ladleful of the beef gravy on top. Top with the fried egg.

煎面

Crispy Chicken Noodles with Gravy

Time
30–40 minutes

Ingredients

For the noodles

4 servings of dried fine egg noodles

5 tsp neutral cooking oil (optional)

For the sauce

1 tbsp oyster sauce

1 tsp light soy sauce

1 tsp sesame oil

½ tsp salt

pinch of ground white pepper

1¼ cups (300 ml) water or stock (any kind)

For the gravy

1 tbsp neutral cooking oil

½ carrot, julienned

3 scallions, cut into thirds

3 dried shiitake mushrooms, rehydrated and thinly sliced

3½ oz (100 g) chicken breast, very thinly sliced into strips

3½ oz (100 g) beansprouts

For the cornstarch slurry

1 tbsp cornstarch

3 tbsp water

This is the dish that my British partner fell in love with when he moved to Hong Kong. When we go to our local Cantonese café for lunch, he will *always* order this dish of shatteringly crispy egg noodles topped with a delicious gravy. Usually made with pork, I use chicken because you can easily make this dish with leftover shredded chicken. Making the crispy noodles isn't difficult, it just takes a bit of time. If you prefer, you can skip the crispy noodles and simply enjoy the sauce with boiled noodles.

Place the noodles in a large bowl and cover with boiling water. Leave to soak for 6–8 minutes, or until soft with a slight bite. Drain and leave to steam-dry in a colander for 5 minutes. Once slightly cooled, toss the cooked noodles with 1 teaspoon of the cooking oil. You can leave them as they are at this point, or go on to make them crispy.

To make the crispy noodles, heat 2 teaspoons of the oil in a large nonstick frying pan over medium heat. Add the noodles and spread into a thin layer, pressing down with a spatula to flatten them. Cook, without moving them, for 4–6 minutes until golden brown. Place a large heatproof plate on top of the pan, then flip the noodles onto the plate. Side the noodles back into the pan, crispy-side up. Drizzle the remaining 2 teaspoons of oil around the edges of the noodles and cook for a further 4–6 minutes until golden brown. Transfer to a serving plate.

In a small bowl, mix together the ingredients for the sauce.

For the gravy, heat the oil in a wok or pan over high heat. Add the carrot and scallions and cook for 2–3 minutes. Add the mushrooms, chicken and sauce around the edges of the pan. Bring to a boil, then reduce the heat to low and simmer for 3–4 minutes until the chicken is almost cooked through. At the last minute, stir in the beansprouts.

In a small bowl, mix together the ingredients for the cornstarch slurry. Slowly add it to the gravy while continuously stirring. Boil for 1–2 minutes until thickened. Taste to adjust the seasonings.

Ladle the gravy evenly over the noodles and serve.

Serves 4

大排面
Fried Pork Chop with Soup Noodles

Time

25 minutes, plus 20 minutes marinating

Ingredients

4 boneless pork chops

⅔ cup (70 g) cornstarch

1 tbsp neutral cooking oil

4 servings of thin wheat noodles

7 oz (200 g) bok choi, cut in half lengthways

For the marinade

1 tbsp oyster sauce

2 tsp sesame oil

1 tsp salt

1 tsp sugar

For the soup

2 tsp neutral cooking oil

1 large piece of fresh ginger root, peeled and thinly sliced into discs

4 scallions, cut into thirds

2 tbsp dark soy sauce

4 tbsp light soy sauce

½ tsp sugar

4¼ cups (1 liter) water or stock (any kind)

Walking around the streets of Shanghai, you'll see many noodle shops serving this dish—a delicious pork chop served with noodles in soup. The direct translation is "big chop noodle." The pork chops are fried, then coated in a delicious soy-based sauce. Add a bit more water to the sauce and there you have the soup for your noodles. Simple as that.

Place the pork chops on a chopping board. Using the back edge of a knife or a meat tenderizer, bash the chops into cutlets about ½ in (1 cm) thick. Cut small indents into the curved edge of each chop, so they remain flat while frying. Place in a bowl and add the marinade ingredients. Gently massage for 2–3 minutes. Leave to marinate for at least 20 minutes.

For the soup, heat the oil in a large pan over high heat. Add the ginger and most of the scallions (save some, thinly sliced, for garnish), and cook for 2–3 minutes until fragrant. Add the dark soy sauce, light soy sauce, salt, sugar and 1⅔ cups (400 ml) of the measured water. Bring to a boil, then reduce the heat to low and simmer while you prepare the rest of the components.

Meanwhile, spread the cornstarch over a large shallow plate. Add the pork and turn to coat evenly.

Heat the oil in a large frying pan over medium-high heat. Add the pork and cook for 6–8 minutes until golden brown and cooked through. Place on a plate lined with paper towels or a cooling rack to drain.

Bring a large pot of water to a boil. Add the noodles and cook according to the package instructions. In the last 2–3 minutes, add the bok choi to the pot. Drain, then transfer the cooked noodles and bok choi to serving bowls.

Dip the cooked pork chops in the soup mixture, then place on top of the noodles.

Add the remaining 2½ cups (600 ml) water to the soup mixture and bring to a boil. Taste to adjust the seasonings. Divide the broth among the noodle bowls, garnish with the reserved scallions and serve.

Fried Rice 5 Ways

Tips

1. Use leftover, day-old, cooked rice for the best results. Leftover rice absorbs more seasoning and stays crispy in the pan, while fresh rice tends to get soggy.
2. Wait for the wok/pan to get smoking hot before adding any ingredients.
3. Break up any large clumps of rice by pressing them against the sides of the pan with the back of a spatula.
4. Do not overmix the rice while stir-frying. Spread it out evenly and give it a few minutes to cook undisturbed.
5. Run the spatula in a criss-cross shape across the wok/pan, scraping the bottom of the rice and sweeping in an upwards motion.

---

1. Classic Egg Fried Rice VG

Ingredients

2 tsp neutral cooking oil

1 egg

2 servings (about 3¾ cups/600 g) of cooked and cooled jasmine rice (see Tips, above)

2 scallions, thinly sliced

2 tsp sesame oil

2 tsp light soy sauce

pinch of salt

pinch of ground white pepper

Heat the oil in a wok or frying pan over high heat. Crack in the egg and scramble for 1–2 minutes, running a spatula across the egg.

Add the rice and spread it out into an even layer. Leave to cook for 1–2 minutes undisturbed.

Breaking up any clumps with the back of the spatula, cook for a further 3–5 minutes, tossing vigorously to combine.

Add half of the scallions and toss.

Add the sesame oil, light soy sauce, salt and white pepper, and toss to combine. Taste to adjust the seasoning.

Transfer to a large serving dish and garnish with the remaining scallions.

2. Not-So-Classic Egg Fried Rice VG

Ingredients

2 servings (about 3¾ cups/600 g) of cooked and cooled jasmine rice (see Tips, page 55)

1 egg

pinch of salt

pinch of ground white pepper

2 tsp neutral cooking oil

2 scallions, thinly sliced

2 tsp sesame oil

2 tsp light soy sauce

Place the rice in a mixing bowl. Crack in the egg and mix until evenly combined. Season with salt and white pepper.

Heat the oil in a wok or frying pan over high heat. Add the rice and spread it out into an even layer. Leave to cook for 1–2 minutes undisturbed. Breaking up any clumps with the back of the spatula, cook for a further 3–5 minutes, tossing vigorously to combine.

Add half of the scallions and toss.

Add the sesame oil and light soy sauce, and toss to combine. Taste to adjust the seasoning.

Transfer to a large serving dish and garnish with the remaining scallions.

---

3. Shrimp and Egg White Fried Rice PESC

Ingredients

4 tsp neutral cooking oil

3 oz (80 g) raw shelled shrimp, cut into ½ in (1 cm) pieces

2 egg whites (yolks for garnish, optional)

2 servings (about 3¾ cups/600 g) cooked and cooled jasmine rice (see Tips, page 55)

2 scallions, thinly sliced

2 tsp sesame oil

2 tsp light soy sauce

pinch of salt

pinch of ground white pepper

Heat 2 teaspoons of the oil in a wok or frying pan over high heat. Add the shrimp and cook for 3–4 minutes until almost cooked. Transfer to a plate and set aside.

Reheat the wok/pan over high heat and add the remaining 2 teaspoons of oil. Add the egg whites and scramble for 1–2 minutes, running a spatula across the egg.

Add the rice and cook for 3–5 minutes, breaking up any clumps with the back of the spatula and tossing vigorously to combine.

Add the shrimp back to the pan along with half of the scallions and toss.

Add the sesame oil, light soy sauce, salt and white pepper, and toss to combine. Taste to adjust the seasoning.

Transfer to a serving dish and garnish with the remaining scallions.

Note

Optional: To avoid waste and for extra deliciousness, top each serving with a raw egg yolk. If doing this, make sure to use high-quality eggs that are safe to consume raw.

4. Bacon and Ketchup Fried Rice

Ingredients

1 tsp neutral cooking oil

1¾ oz (50 g) bacon, chopped

1 egg

2 servings (about 3¾ cups/600 g) of cooked and cooled jasmine rice (see Tips, page 55)

2 scallions, thinly sliced

2 tsp sesame oil

2 tsp light soy sauce

2 tsp ketchup (optional)

pinch of salt

pinch of ground white pepper

Add the oil and the chopped bacon to a wok or frying pan, set over medium heat and cook for 3–4 minutes until some of the fat has rendered out of the bacon.

Crack in the egg and scramble for 1–2 minutes, running a spatula across the egg.

Add the rice and spread it out into an even layer. Leave to cook for 1–2 minutes undisturbed. Breaking up any clumps with the back of the spatula, cook for a further 3–5 minutes, tossing vigorously to combine.

Add half of the scallions and toss.

Add the sesame oil, light soy sauce, ketchup, salt and white pepper, and toss to combine. Taste to adjust the seasoning.

Transfer to a serving dish and garnish with the remaining scallions.

---

5. Garlic Fried Rice VG

Ingredients

4 tsp neutral cooking oil

1 egg

5 garlic cloves, finely chopped

2 servings (about 3¾ cups/600 g) of cooked and cooled jasmine rice (see Tips, page 55)

2 scallions, thinly sliced

2 tsp sesame oil

2 tsp light soy sauce

pinch of salt

pinch of ground white pepper

Heat 1 teaspoon of the oil in a wok or frying pan over high heat. Crack in the egg and scramble for 1–2 minutes, running a spatula across the egg. Transfer to a plate and set aside.

Add the remaining 3 teaspoons of oil to the pan, along with the garlic, and cook over medium-low heat for 5–6 minutes until light golden brown.

Add the rice and spread it out into an even layer. Leave to cook for 1–2 minutes undisturbed.

Breaking up any clumps with the back of the spatula, cook for a further 3–5 minutes, tossing vigorously to combine.

Add the scrambled egg back to the pan along with half of the scallions and toss.

Add the sesame oil, light soy sauce, salt and white pepper, and toss to combine. Taste to adjust the seasoning.

Transfer to a serving dish and garnish with the remaining scallions.

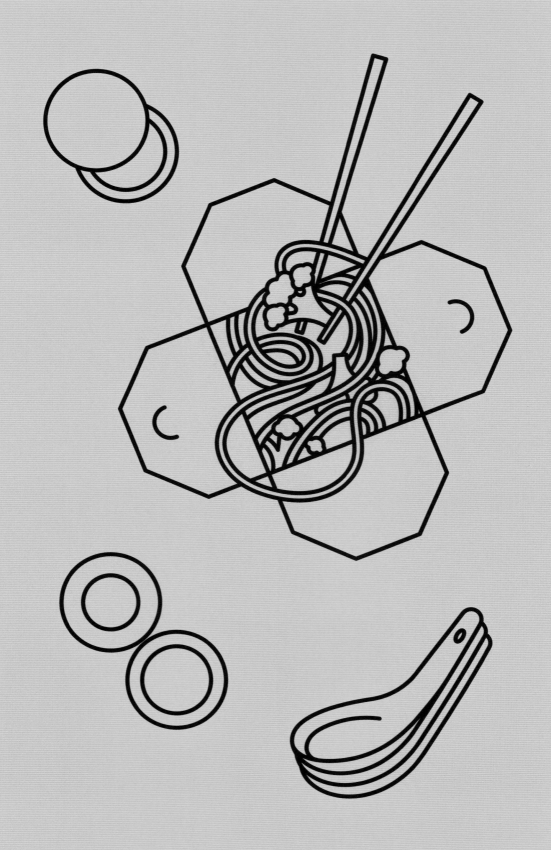

chapter

takeout at home

two

菠萝咕噜肉
Sweet and Sour Pork

A quintessential Chinese takeout dish, this crispy sweet and sour pork has won the hearts of many Hong Kongers. Traditionally, the pork is deep-fried twice to make it extra crispy. I've included an air-fryer option, which makes cooking it so much easier. Usually, quite a bit of sugar is used to balance the sour flavor. However, my recipe uses the natural sweetness in canned pineapple juice.

Time

30–40 minutes, plus 20 minutes or overnight marinating

Ingredients

1 lb (500 g) pork shoulder, cut into ¾ in (2 cm) cubes

neutral cooking oil, for frying

½ red pepper, cut into ¾ in (2 cm) cubes

½ green pepper, cut into ¾ in (2 cm) cubes

1 white onion, cu into ¾ in (2 cm) cubes

8 oz (225 g) canned pineapple, drained, cut into ¾ in (2 cm) chunks (reserve the juice for the sauce)

For the marinade

2 tsp light soy sauce

½ tsp sugar

1 tbsp Shaoxing rice wine

½ tsp baking soda

1 egg

For the sauce

½ cup (120 g) ketchup

6 tbsp white rice vinegar (or any light-colored vinegar)

¼ cup (60 ml) pineapple juice

1½ tbsp oyster sauce (or mushroom stir-fry sauce)

½ tsp salt

For the coating

1⅓ cups (150 g) cornstarch

1 tsp ground white pepper

1 tsp salt

1 tbsp baking powder

Place the pork in a large bowl and add the marinade ingredients. Mix to combine, massaging the pork for 2–3 minutes. Leave to marinate for at least 20 minutes, or overnight in the fridge.

In a small bowl, mix together the ingredients for the sauce.

In a large bowl, mix together the ingredients for the coating. In batches, remove the pork from the marinade and place into the coating mixture. Toss to evenly coat. Shake off any excess and place the coated pork on a large plate or tray.

To air-fry:

Preheat the air fryer to 400°F (200°C). Place the coated pork onto an air-fryer pan pan lined with parchment paper, leaving plenty of space in between. Spray with cooking oil and air-fry for 16–18 minutes, flipping halfway, until deep golden brown and cooked through.

To deep-fry:

Fill a deep pan or wok halfway with cooking oil and set over medium heat. When the oil is hot enough (see note), gently lower the pork into the hot oil, in batches. Cook for 4–6 minutes until the pork is cooked through and light golden brown. Drain on a wire rack. Repeat with the remaining pork.

For the second deep-fry, turn the heat up to high. In batches, lower the pork into the oil and cook for 1–2 minutes, or until the pork is amber brown. Transfer to a plate lined with paper towels. Set aside.

Heat 1 tablespoon of oil in a large wok or frying pan over high heat. Add the peppers, onion and pineapple, and cook for 3–4 minutes until slightly charred. Add the fried pork and toss to combine. Pour the sauce around the edges of the pan—it should immediately sizzle. Cook for 2–3 minutes, tossing to combine, until the pork is evenly coated. Transfer to a large plate and serve.

Notes

To test if the oil is hot enough, insert a wooden chopstick into the oil. If it immediately sizzles, then the oil is hot enough. While deep-frying, if the oil gets too hot, reduce the heat or add a small splash of cold oil to bring the temperature down quickly.

Chinese chefs and home cooks often use baking soda to tenderize meat. This process is called "velveting." Some people only add baking soda, while others also add egg white, cornstarch and oil to get silky, tender meat. You only need a small amount of baking soda to achieve velvet-tender meat—too much will affect the flavor.

Serves 2

豉油皇炒面

Hong Kong Stir-Fried Noodles VG

Time

10–15 minutes

Ingredients

2 tsp plus 1 tbsp neutral cooking oil

4 scallions, cut into thirds, then cut in half lengthways

2 oz (60 g) Chinese chives, cut into thirds (omit if you can't find any)

5¼ oz (150 g) beansprouts, rinsed

½ tsp salt, or to taste

2 servings of cooked fine egg noodles (see Note)

2 tsp light soy sauce

2 tsp dark soy sauce

pinch of ground white pepper

The name of this dish literally translates to "soy sauce queen stir-fried noodles." It's a famous Hong Kong dish served in almost all local restaurants and many Chinese takeout restaurants around the world. A seemingly simple dish with only a few ingredients, the secret to achieving that famous crispy noodle texture is in the technique.

Heat 2 teaspoons of the oil in a large frying pan or wok over high heat. Add the scallions and cook for 2–3 minutes until fragrant. Add the chives and beansprouts, and cook for 2–3 minutes until slightly softened. Season with salt, then transfer to a large plate and set aside.

Reheat the pan/wok with the tablespoon of oil over high heat.

Add the noodles and spread into a thin layer. Cook for 3–4 minutes, undisturbed, until they are getting crispy. Toss and shake up the noodles, then spread into a thin layer again. Cook for a further 3–4 minutes until crispy. Return the vegetables to the pan, add the light and dark soy sauces, and toss to combine. Season with the salt and white pepper.

Transfer to a large plate and serve.

Notes

Below are the different preparations for various types of egg noodles.

Dried egg noodles:

Place the noodles into a large bowl and cover with boiling water. Leave to soak for 6–8 minutes, or until the noodles are soft with a slight bite. You want the noodles to be slightly underdone so they retain their texture after stir-frying. Drain, then transfer to a large plate or tray lined with a tea towel. Leave to steam-dry for 8–10 minutes. Once dry, toss lightly with cooking oil to prevent the noodles from sticking.

Uncooked fresh egg noodles:

Place the noodles in a pot of boiling water and cook according to the package instructions (usually around 2–3 minutes) until soft with a slight bite. Drain, then repeat the drying steps, as above.

Cooked egg noodles:

Place the noodles into a large bowl and break up any clumps. If the noodles feel sticky, lightly toss with cooking oil.

Serves 4

干炒牛河
Beef Chow Fun

Time
25–30 minutes

Ingredients

1 lb 7 oz (650 g) beef steak (flank or skirt), very thinly sliced into ¾ in (2 cm) wide strips

2 tbsp neutral cooking oil

4 scallions, cut into thirds, then halved lengthways

7 oz (200 g) beansprouts, rinsed

1¾ oz (50 g) Chinese chives, cut into thirds (omit if you can't find any)

14 oz (400 g) cooked ½ in (1 cm) wide rice noodles (or around 4½ oz/125 g dried—see Note)

For the marinade
½ tsp sugar

½ tsp baking soda

2 tsp light soy sauce

2 tbsp water

2 tsp cornstarch

pinch of ground white pepper

For the sauce
2 tbsp light soy sauce

1 tbsp dark soy sauce

1 tsp sugar

pinch of ground white pepper

This is one of my all-time favorite Hong Kong noodle dishes. The beef is silky and tender and the rice noodles absorb all the sauce. The name of this dish literally translates to "dry stir-fry noodle," because its cooked quickly over high heat to prevent the beef and noodles from overcooking. If you can, try to seek out fresh rice noodles. They're an affordable ingredient most often sold in the chilled aisle of Asian supermarkets and make all the difference in a simple dish like this.

Place the beef in a medium bowl and add the marinade ingredients. Massage for 1–2 minutes, then leave to marinate for at least 10 minutes.

In a small bowl, mix together the ingredients for the sauce.

Heat 1 tablespoon of the oil in a large wok or frying pan over high heat. Add the marinated beef, spreading it out into a thin layer, and cook for 3–4 minutes, undisturbed. Flip and cook for 1–2 minutes on the other side until almost cooked through. Transfer to a plate and set aside.

Reheat the wok or pan with the other tablespoon of oil over high heat. Add the scallions and cook for 1–2 minutes, then add the beansprouts and chives, and cook for 2–3 minutes. Add the noodles and toss to combine with two spatulas or chopsticks.

Return the beef to the pan. Add the sauce around the edges of the pan and toss vigorously to combine. Cook for 2–3 minutes until the noodles have absorbed all the sauce (the stir-fry should be quite dry). Taste to adjust the seasonings.

Transfer to a large plate and serve.

Note
If using dried rice noodles, place in a large bowl and cover with boiling water. Leave to soak for 5–7 minutes until the noodles are soft with a slight bite. You want the noodles to be slightly underdone so they retain their texture after stir-frying. Drain, then transfer to a large colander. Leave to steam-dry for 5–7 minutes. Once dry, toss lightly with cooking oil to prevent the noodles from sticking to each other.

Serves 4

炒面
Chow Mein VG

Time

15 minutes

Ingredients

2 tsp plus 1 tbsp neutral cooking oil

¼ cabbage, thinly sliced

½ onion, thinly sliced

1 carrot, thinly sliced into matchsticks

3 scallions, sliced into thirds

5¼ oz (150 g) beansprouts, rinsed

salt, to taste

3 servings of cooked egg noodles (see Note on page 65)

For the sauce

1 tbsp light soy sauce

2 tsp dark soy sauce

2 tsp sesame oil

2 tsp mushroom stir-fry sauce

½ tsp sugar

pinch of ground white pepper

There are so many varieties of chow mein, as it simply means "stir-fried noodles." This is essentially a saucier version of Hong Kong Stir-Fried Noodles (page 65) with added vegetables. The trick with any noodle stir-fry is to not overcrowd the pan—this gives the ingredients more space to be in contact with heat, thus cook quicker and get crispier (and avoiding soggy mush). You can use whatever vegetables you have on hand, just make sure to slice them into long, thin strands so they mix well with the noodles. *Pictured overleaf.*

In a small bowl, mix the ingredients for the sauce.

Heat 2 teaspoons of the oil in a large frying pan or wok over high heat. Add the cabbage, onion and carrot, and cook for 3–4 minutes until softening. Add the scallions and beansprouts, and cook for 2–3 minutes until softening. Season with salt, then transfer to a plate and set aside.

Reheat the pan/wok with the tablespoon of oil over high heat. Add the noodles and cook for 3–4 minutes until starting to crisp up. Return the vegetables to the pan, add the sauce around the edges of the pan and toss vigorously to combine. Taste to adjust the seasonings.

Transfer to a large plate and serve immediately.

西兰花炒牛肉

Beef and Broccoli Stir-Fry

Time
25–30 minutes

Ingredients

9 oz (250 g) beef steak (flank or skirt), thinly sliced into ¾ in (2 cm) wide strips

1 small head of broccoli

pinch of salt

1 tbsp neutral cooking oil

1 small piece of fresh ginger root, peeled and cut into thin discs

3 garlic cloves, crushed

2 scallions, sliced into thirds

For the marinade

½ tsp baking soda

1 tbsp oyster sauce

1 tsp light soy sauce

2 tsp cornstarch

pinch of ground white pepper

½ tsp sugar

1 tbsp Shaoxing rice wine

1 tbsp water

For the sauce

1 tbsp oyster sauce

1 tsp light soy sauce

2 tsp dark soy sauce

1 tbsp Shaoxing rice wine

½ tsp sugar

pinch of ground white pepper

2 tsp cornstarch

1 tbsp water

Serves 4

I grew up with so many variations of this homestyle Cantonese dish, where different seasonal vegetables are stir-fried with pork or chicken. Here, the beef is smooth and tender, while the broccoli is crunchy and covered in a silky glaze. The variations of this recipe are endless—an excellent way to use up different bits in the fridge. *Pictured overleaf.*

Place the beef in a medium bowl and add the ingredients for the marinade. Mix to combine. Leave to marinate for at least 10 minutes.

Remove the stalk from the broccoli and cut the head into roughly 1½ in (4 cm) florets. Peel the stalk and cut into ¾ in (2 cm) wide strips, a similar size to the beef strips.

In a small bowl, mix together the ingredients for the sauce (see Note).

Fill a wok or pot with water and bring to a boil. Add a pinch of salt, then add the broccoli stalk and cook for 1–2 minutes. Add the florets and cook for 2–3 minutes, then drain and set aside.

Reheat the wok or pot with the oil over high heat. Add the ginger, garlic and scallions, and cook for 1–2 minutes until fragrant. Add the beef and all its marinade to the pan, spread into a thin layer and cook for 2–3 minutes without moving it, then flip and cook for another 2–3 minutes until golden brown.

Return the broccoli to the pan and mix to combine. Add the sauce around the edges of the pan, toss vigorously and cook for 1–2 minutes until the sauce thickens and coats the vegetables and beef.

Transfer to a large plate and serve.

Note

A very simple tip, but whenever I add cornstarch to a sauce, I always leave the spoon I used to mix the sauce in the bowl. That way, I can give the sauce a quick mix before adding it to the pan, as cornstarch tends to sink to the bottom.

Serves 2

柠檬鸡
Lemon Chicken

Time

30 minutes, plus 20 minutes or overnight marinating

Ingredients

10½ oz (300 g) chicken breast, cut into small bite-sized chunks

neutral cooking oil, for frying

For the marinade

pinch of ground white pepper

½ tsp salt

1 tsp light soy sauce

1 tbsp Shaoxing rice wine (optional)

zest of 1 lemon

2 tsp cornstarch

1 egg, beaten

For the sauce

⅓ cup (80 ml) water

3 tbsp honey

juice of 1 lemon

½ tsp salt

1 tsp light soy sauce

For the cornstarch slurry

1 tbsp cornstarch

3½ tbsp water

For the coating

scant 1 cup (100 g) cornstarch

1 tbsp baking powder

1 tsp salt

1 tsp ground white pepper

¼ tsp ground turmeric (optional, for color)

These crispy bites of tender chicken coated in a tangy lemon sauce are irresistible. I use honey in my recipe because it adds a gentle sweetness to the lemon sauce. The balance of sweet and sour is really up to you—feel free to adjust the quantities to your own tastes. If you like your dish on the sour side, add more lemon juice; if you like it sweeter, add more honey.

Place the chicken in a large bowl and add the marinade ingredients. Leave to marinate for at least 20 minutes, or overnight in the fridge.

Place the sauce ingredients in a large frying pan or wok and bring to a boil.

In a small bowl, mix together the ingredients for the cornstarch slurry.

Once the sauce is boiling, reduce the heat to low. Slowly add the cornstarch slurry, while continuously stirring. Boil for 1–2 minutes until thickened, then remove from the heat. Taste to adjust the seasoning.

In a large bowl, mix together the coating ingredients.

In batches, remove the chicken from the marinade and place it into the coating. Toss, pressing the mixture into the chicken to evenly coat. Shake off any excess and place on a large plate or tray.

Note

To test if the oil is hot enough, insert a wooden chopstick/utensil into the oil. If it immediately sizzles, then the oil is hot enough. While deep-frying, if the oil gets too hot, reduce the heat or add a small splash of cold oil to bring the temperature down quickly.

To air-fry:

Preheat the air fryer to 400°F (200°C). Place the chicken on an air-fryer pan lined with parchment paper and spray with cooking oil. Air-fry for 14–16 minutes, flipping halfway, until golden brown and cooked through.

To deep-fry:

Fill a large pan or wok halfway with cooking oil and set over medium heat (see note). In batches and with a large slotted spoon, gently lower the chicken into the oil. Deep-fry for 4–6 minutes until cooked through and a light golden brown. Transfer to a wire rack. Repeat with the remaining chicken.

For the second deep-fry, turn the heat up to high. In batches, lower the chicken into the oil and cook for 1–2 minutes, or until golden brown. Transfer to a plate or tray lined with paper towels and set aside.

Add the cooked chicken to the sauce and toss to combine. Place on a serving platter and serve immediately.

蛋花汤
Egg Drop Soup VG

A classic comfort food that comes together in 10 minutes or less. In Chinese, this dish is called "egg flower soup" because the eggs open like flowers once poured into the soup. My simple trick for getting those beautiful wispy eggs? Add a splash of water to the beaten eggs to help them cook evenly and achieve those long silky strands. You can easily double this recipe to serve four, if you like.

Time
10 minutes

Ingredients
generous 2 cups (500 ml) high-quality, low-sodium chicken stock

½ tsp salt

1 tsp light soy sauce

1 tsp sesame oil

1 scallion, thinly sliced

pinch of ground white pepper

For the egg mixture
2 eggs

1 tbsp water

¼ tsp salt

For the cornstarch slurry
1½ tbsp cornstarch

3 tbsp water

Place the chicken stock into a medium pot and bring to a boil.

Crack the eggs into a small bowl and add the water and salt. Whisk until no bits of egg white remain.

In a small bowl, mix together the ingredients for the cornstarch slurry.

Reduce the heat under the stock to a simmer. Slowly add the cornstarch slurry while continuously stirring. Boil for 1–2 minutes until thickened.

Reduce the heat to low again. Add the salt, light soy sauce and sesame oil. Steadily pour in the eggs in a thin stream while slowly stirring with chopsticks or a spatula. Taste to adjust the seasoning.

Serve in bowls, garnished with the scallion.

Serves 2-4

干煸牛肉
Crispy Chile Beef

Time
30 minutes

Ingredients

14 oz (400 g) tenderloin or sirloin steak, very thinly sliced into shreds

neutral cooking oil, for frying

½ onion, thinly sliced

½ red bell pepper, thinly sliced

2 garlic cloves, finely chopped

1 large red chile, thinly sliced

For the marinade
1 tsp baking soda

2 tsp light soy sauce

½ tsp sugar

1 tbsp Shaoxing rice wine

1 egg, beaten

For the sauce
4 tbsp Thai sweet chile sauce

1 tbsp light soy sauce

2 tsp dark soy sauce

1 tbsp black rice vinegar

2 tsp honey

2 tsp sesame oil

2 tsp Sriracha sauce

For the coating
1 cup (120 g) cornstarch

1 tbsp baking powder

1 tsp salt

1 tsp ground white pepper

The exact orgins of this dish are unknown, but some believe it may come from a Sichuanese dish of beef strips stir-fried with plenty of chile. The takeout version has more sauce, and the secret to mine is Sriracha, which adds just a bit of heat and tang to complement the beef. For a spicier version, feel free to stir-fry the beef with the fresh chile rather than using it just as a garnish.

Place the beef in a medium bowl and add the ingredients for the marinade. Mix to combine, massaging with your hands for 2-3 minutes. Leave to marinate for at least 15 minutes.

In a small bowl, mix together the ingredients for the sauce. Taste to adjust the seasonings.

In a separate small bowl, mix together the ingredients for the coating.

In batches, remove the beef from the marinade and place into the coating mixture. Toss to evenly coat, then shake off any excess and place the coated beef on a large plate or tray.

To air-fry:
Preheat the air fryer to 400°F (200°C). Place the beef on an air-fryer pan lined with parchment paper and spray with cooking oil. Air-fry for 6-7 minutes until crispy and cooked through.

To shallow-fry:
Cover the bottom of a frying pan or wok with a thin layer of cooking oil and set over medium heat. In batches, add the beef and cook for 4-6 minutes, turning to make sure all sides are golden and crispy. Transfer to a wire rack and set aside.

Heat 2 teaspoons of oil in a large wok or frying pan over high heat. Add the onion and pepper, and cook for 2-3 minutes until softening. Add the garlic and cook for 1 minute. Pour the sauce around the edges of the pan—it should sizzle immediately. Add the beef and quickly toss to combine.

Transfer to a large plate, garnish with the chile and serve.

Note
Chinese chefs and home cooks often use baking soda to tenderize meat. This process is called "velveting." Some people only add baking soda, while others also add egg white, cornstarch and oil to get silky, tender meat. You only need a small amount of baking soda to achieve velvet-tender meat—too much will affect the flavor.

担担面
Dan Dan Noodles VE

Time
15 minutes

Ingredients

2 tsp neutral cooking oil

7 oz (200 g) fresh mushrooms (any variety), finely chopped (or 6 dried shiitake mushrooms, rehydrated)

2 scallions, finely chopped (white and green parts separated)

2 garlic cloves, minced

1 tbsp Shaoxing rice wine

1 tsp light soy sauce

2 tbsp water (or mushroom soaking liquid)

2 servings of thin wheat noodles

½ tsp crushed or ground Sichuan peppercorns (optional but recommended)

salt and ground white pepper

For the sauce

2 tbsp Chinese sesame paste (see page 15) or peanut butter

2 tsp light soy sauce

2 tsp sesame oil

2 tbsp black rice vinegar

2–3 tsp chile oil, or more to taste

1 garlic clove, minced

½ tsp sugar

If you're walking through the streets of Chengdu, you'll see countless noodle shops selling dan dan noodles—a mixed noodle served at room temperature, topped with ground pork and a spicy nutty sauce. My version is vegan and I use mushrooms instead. I've given you an option to use fresh mushrooms or rehydrated dried shiitake mushrooms. The two give slightly different results. You can also use a mixture of both, if you prefer.

Heat the oil in a large wok or frying pan over medium-high heat. Add the mushrooms and fry for 4–6 minutes until cooked. Add the scallion whites, garlic, rice wine, light soy sauce, water and a pinch of salt and white pepper. Mix and taste to adjust the seasonings. Remove from the heat and set aside.

In a small bowl, mix together the ingredients for the sauce.

Bring a large pot of water to a boil. Add the noodles and cook according to the package instructions. Towards the end of cooking, add around ⅓ cup (80 ml) of the noodle cooking water to the sauce and mix. For a thinner sauce, add more noodle cooking water. Drain the noodles, then rinse under cold water to stop the cooking process.

Divide the noodles between serving bowls. Evenly pour over the sauce and top with the mushrooms, scallion greens and the crushed Sichuan peppercorns. Drizzle with more chile oil, to taste, and serve. Make sure to give the noodles a good mix in the sauce before digging in.

Serves 2

麻婆豆腐
Mapo Tofu ^{VE}

This is one of my all-time favorite Chinese dishes. I've ordered this at so many Chinese restaurants and no two places ever prepare it the same way. Traditionally, the recipe uses ground pork and the key ingredient is chile bean paste. My version is vegan-friendly, because its a dish everyone should be able to enjoy. It's also slightly milder, but feel free to make it spicier by adding more dried chiles and chile oil.

Time
15–20 minutes

Ingredients

14 oz (400 g) silken tofu, cut into ¾ in (2 cm) cubes

2 tsp neutral cooking oil

1 tbsp chile bean paste

3 garlic cloves, finely chopped

1 small piece of fresh ginger root, peeled and finely chopped

4 scallions, thinly sliced (white and green parts separated)

4 dried shiitake mushrooms, rehydrated and finely chopped or thinly sliced

1–2 tsp crushed or ground Sichuan peppercorns

2–4 whole dried red chiles (optional)

salt

For the sauce

1¼ cups (300 ml) mushroom soaking liquid (or water/vegetable stock)

1 tbsp Shaoxing rice wine

2 tsp black rice vinegar, or more to taste

2 tsp light soy sauce

1 tsp dark soy sauce

1–2 tsp chile oil, or more to taste

1 tsp sesame oil

1 tsp sugar

½ tsp ground white pepper

For the cornstarch slurry

1 tbsp cornstarch

2 tbsp water

Place the diced tofu into a large bowl, add a pinch of salt and cover with boiling water. Set aside.

In a small bowl, mix together the ingredients for the sauce.

In a small bowl, mix together the ingredients for the cornstarch slurry.

Heat the oil in a wok or pot over high heat. Add the chile bean paste and cook for 2–3 minutes until sizzling. Add the garlic, ginger and scallion whites, and cook for 1–2 minutes. Add the mushrooms, Sichuan peppercorns and chiles (if using) and mix to combine. Add the sauce around the edges of the pot and cook for 1–2 minutes. Drain the tofu then gently add it to the pot. Reduce the heat to medium and cook for 3–4 minutes until the sauce has slightly reduced.

Reduce the heat to a simmer, then slowly add the cornstarch slurry while continuously stirring. Boil for 1–2 minutes until thickened, then taste to adjust the seasonings.

Transfer to a shallow serving bowl and garnish with the scallion greens.

Serves 4

宫保鸡丁
Kung Pao Chicken

Coming from the Sichuan region of China, this dish is well-loved around the world. Traditionally, Chinese chefs fry the Sichuan peppercorns, dried chiles and peanuts separately to bring out their aromas. In my recipe, the chicken and spices are fried together so you get all the flavor, with a lot less work. My version is more similar to one you would find in a restaurant in China, rather than the takeout-style.

Time

15 minutes, plus 15 minutes or overnight marinating

Ingredients

1 lb 7 oz (650 g) chicken breast, cut into small cubes

1 tbsp neutral cooking oil

4 scallions (white parts only), cut into ½ in (1 cm) cubes

1 large piece of fresh ginger root, peeled and cut into ½ in (1 cm) cubes

3 garlic cloves, crushed

⅓ cup (50 g) whole peanuts

1-2 dried chiles, cut into ½ in (1 cm) cubes (optional)

1 tsp Sichuan peppercorns (optional)

For the marinade

2 tsp Shaoxing rice wine

1 tsp light soy sauce

½ tsp baking soda

1 tsp sugar

1 tbsp cornstarch

pinch of ground white pepper

1 egg, beaten

For the sauce

1 tbsp Shaoxing rice wine

2 tsp oyster sauce

2 tsp black rice vinegar

2 tsp light soy sauce

1 tsp dark soy sauce

1 tsp sugar

Place the chicken in a large bowl and add all the marinade ingredients. Mix to combine. Leave to marinate for at least 15 minutes, or overnight in the fridge.

In a small bowl, mix together the ingredients for the sauce.

Heat the oil in a large wok or frying pan over high heat. Add the scallions, ginger and garlic, and cook for 1-2 minutes. Drain the chicken from the marinade, add it to the pan and cook for 3-4 minutes until golden brown, then flip and cook for another 2-3 minutes. Add the peanuts, dried chiles and Sichuan peppercorns (if using), and cook for 1-2 minutes until fragrant. Add the sauce around the edges of the pan and cook for 2-3 minutes until most of the sauce has evaporated and the chicken is cooked through.

Transfer to a large plate and serve.

Serves 2

棒棒虾
Bang Bang Shrimp PESC

Time
20 minutes

Ingredients
6 oz (165 g) raw shelled shrimp

neutral cooking oil, for frying

For the marinade
pinch of ground white pepper

1 tsp light soy sauce

2 tsp Shaoxing rice wine

1 tsp cornstarch

1 tsp sesame oil

1 egg, beaten

For the coating
scant 1 cup (100 g) cornstarch

1 tbsp baking powder

1 tsp salt

1 tsp ground white pepper

1 tsp garlic powder (optional)

1 tsp onion powder (optional)

¼ tsp ground turmeric (optional, for color)

For the sauce
2 tsp honey

1 tbsp apple cider vinegar (or any light-colored vinegar)

3 tbsp mayonnaise

1 tbsp Thai sweet chile sauce

2–3 tsp Sriracha sauce

pinch of ground black pepper

This is my take on a more American-style Chinese takeout dish, typically made with chicken. Crispy bites of perfectly cooked shrimp are coated or dipped in a tangy sauce made with ingredients you probably already have in the fridge. These are so easy to make but look really impressive when served on a large platter for a dinner or party with friends. My recipe uses an air fryer for ease, but you can also shallow-fry.

Place the shrimp in a large mixing bowl and add the ingredients for the marinade. Mix to combine. Leave to marinate while you prepare the rest of the ingredients.

In a large bowl, mix together the ingredients for the coating.

In batches, remove the shrimp from the marinade and place into the coating. Turn to evenly coat. Place the coated shrimp onto an air-fryer pan lined with parchment paper.

To air-fry:
Preheat the air fryer to 400°F (200°C). Spray the shrimp with cooking oil and air-fry for 10–12 minutes until the shrimp are crispy and cooked through.

To shallow-fry:
Cover the bottom of a frying pan or wok with a thin layer of oil and set over medium heat. In batches, gently lower the shrimp into the oil and cook for 4–6 minutes, turning halfway, until golden and crispy. Transfer to a wire rack and set aside.

In a small bowl, mix together the ingredients for the sauce. Taste to adjust the seasonings.

Place the shrimp on a serving platter and serve with the sauce on the side for dipping. Alternatively, place the shrimp into a large mixing bowl and toss with the sauce, then transfer to a plate and serve.

椒盐豆腐
Salt and Pepper Tofu VE

Time
20 minutes

Ingredients

1 x 14 oz (400 g) block of medium-firm tofu, cut into bite-sized cubes

1 tsp salt

neutral cooking oil, for frying

2 shallots, finely chopped

2 scallions, finely chopped

1 large chile, finely chopped (deseeded for less heat)

2 garlic cloves, finely chopped

2 scallions, finely chopped

For the coating

1 cup (120 g) cornstarch

1 tsp salt

1 tsp ground white pepper

1 tbsp baking powder

¼ tsp ground turmeric (optional, for color)

For the seasoning

1 tsp salt

¼ tsp garlic powder

¼ tsp onion powder

¼ tsp ground white pepper

¼ tsp freshly ground black pepper

In Hong Kong, all seafood restaurants will serve a version of "Salt and Pepper." It could be shrimp, squid, or fish. What makes this dish special is the delicious sand-like seasoning that coats every crispy bite. My vegan recipe uses tofu, but you can use this method to "salt and pepper" anything.

Place the tofu in a large mixing bowl, add the salt and cover with boiling water. Set aside while you prepare the rest of the ingredients.

In a large bowl, mix together the ingredients for the coating.

Drain the tofu and gently pat dry. Place the tofu into the coating mixture and turn to evenly coat. Shake off any excess and transfer to a large plate or tray.

To air-fry:

Preheat the air fryer to 425°F (220°C). Place the tofu on an air-fryer pan lined with parchment paper, leaving plenty of space in between each piece. Spray with neutral oil and air-fry for 8–10 minutes until crispy.

To shallow-fry:

Cover the bottom of a frying pan or wok with a thin layer of oil and set over medium heat. In batches, gently lower the tofu into the oil and cook for 4–6 minutes, turning to make sure all sides are golden and crispy. Transfer to a wire rack and set aside.

In a small bowl, mix together the ingredients for the seasoning.

Heat 2 teaspoons of oil in a large wok or frying pan over high heat. Add the shallots and scallions, and cook for 2–3 minutes until softening. Add the chile and garlic, and cook for 1 minute, then add the tofu and toss to combine. Sprinkle in the seasoning (add half first, then taste and add more if you like).

Transfer to a large plate and serve immediately.

Note

Soaking the tofu in salted water helps it to retain its texture and seasons the tofu so it's more flavorful. You can use this method for salt and pepper squid, shrimp, chicken wings, and so on.

酸辣汤
Hot and Sour Soup ^{VG}

This soup is very popular throughout China, but only served in some takeout spots in the West. It's the soup I make when I want something warm that also packs a punch. The spiciness in the soup comes from ground white pepper, which when used in large amounts adds a lovely peppery heat. Feel free to add more or less vinegar depending on how sour you like the soup. I've used two types of dried mushrooms here, but you can substitute with fresh mushrooms.

Time
15 minutes

Ingredients

generous 2 cups (500 ml) water or stock (any kind)

2 dried shiitake mushrooms, rehydrated and thinly sliced

4 pieces of woodear mushrooms, rehydrated and thinly sliced (around 2 g dried woodear mushrooms)

3½ oz (100 g) silken tofu, thinly sliced into batons

2 tbsp black rice vinegar, or more to taste

2 tsp light soy sauce

1 tsp sesame oil

½ tsp sugar

1 tsp ground white pepper, or more or less to taste

handful of fresh cilantro, roughly torn, to garnish

For the cornstarch slurry
1 tbsp cornstarch

3 tbsp water

For the egg mixture
1 egg

1 tbsp water

Place the stock and mushrooms into a medium pot and bring to a boil.

In a small bowl, mix together the ingredients for the cornstarch slurry.

In a separate small bowl, whisk the egg with the water.

Add the tofu to the pot with the mushrooms and gently stir, being careful not to break the tofu apart. Add the black rice vinegar, light soy sauce, sesame oil, sugar and white pepper, and mix.

Reduce the heat to a simmer and pour in the cornstarch slurry while continuously stirring. Boil for 1–2 minutes until thickened. Remove from the heat, then slowly pour in the egg mixture while continuously whisking with a spoon or chopsticks. Bring back to a boil and taste to adjust the seasonings.

Transfer to bowls, garnish with cilantro and serve immediately.

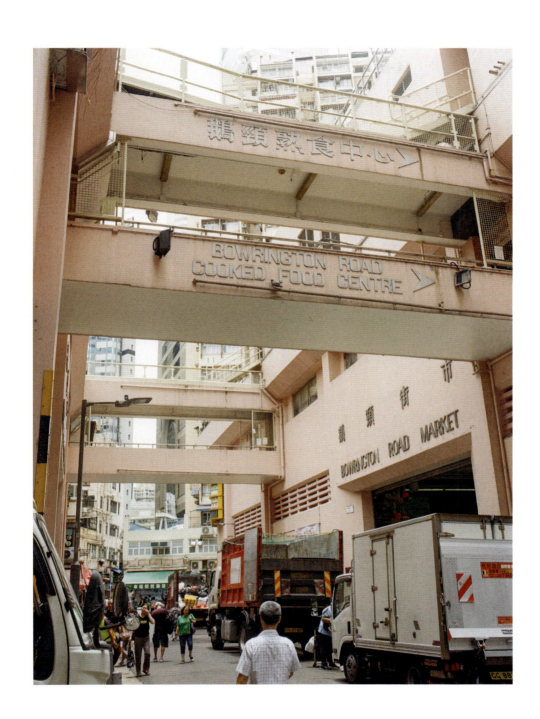

Noodles 5 Ways

凉面

1. Cold Sesame Noodles VG

Nothing quite beats a refreshing bowl of cold noodles on a hot summer's day. There are many varieties of this dish, but this is how the Shanghainese do it—simply topped with cucumber and beansprouts, and drenched in a nutty sesame sauce. I prefer to use thin wheat noodles here because they cling onto the sauce better, but any variety will do. *Pictured overleaf, left.*

Ingredients

- 2 oz (60 g) beansprouts (optional)
- 2 servings of thin wheat noodles
- 1 small cucumber, julienned
- 1 scallion, thinly sliced

For the sauce

- 4 tbsp sesame paste (or peanut butter)
- 4 tbsp black rice vinegar (or any type of vinegar)
- 1½ tbsp light soy sauce
- 1½ tbsp honey
- 1½ tbsp sesame oil
- 1 tbsp Sriracha sauce
- 8–10 tbsp water, or as needed

To garnish

- 1 tsp sesame seeds
- 2 tsp chile oil

Bring a large pot of water to a boil. Add the beansprouts (if using) and cook for 2–3 minutes until softened. Remove with tongs and rinse under cold water. Set aside.

Add the noodles to the same pot and cook according to the package instructions. Drain, then rinse under cold water. Transfer to serving bowls.

In a small bowl, mix together all the ingredients for the sauce and stir until smooth. If the sauce is too thick, add more water.

Top the noodles with the cucumber, scallion and beansprouts (if using). Pour on the sauce and garnish with sesame seeds and a drizzle of chile oil.

豉油拌面

2. Soy and Vinegar Mixed Noodles VE

Ingredients

2 servings of noodles (any kind)

7 oz (200 g) bok choi (or any leafy green)

2 tsp light soy sauce

2 tsp black rice vinegar

2 tsp sesame oil

2 tsp chile oil

½ tsp dark soy sauce

2 scallions, finely chopped, to garnish

These are the noodles I make when I want to do the least amount of dish washing. Everything gets added to the same pan and mixed together. Feel free to add leftover cooked protein, like shredded chicken or firm tofu, to make it a complete meal. Sometimes, I add raw shrimp to the pot when I cook the noodles so they cook at the same time.

Bring a large pot of water to a boil. Add the noodles and cook according to the package instructions. In the last 2–3 minutes of cooking time, add the bok choi to the pot. Drain, then return the noodles and bok choi to the pot.

Add the remaining ingredients, except the scallions, and mix to combine. Taste to adjust the seasoning.

Divide between two bowls and garnish with the scallions.

蒜酱炒面

3. Stir-Fried Spicy Garlic Noodles VE

Ingredients

2 servings of noodles (any kind)

2 garlic cloves, finely chopped

2 scallions, finely chopped

1 tbsp light soy sauce

1 tbsp black rice vinegar

2 tsp dark soy sauce

2–3 tsp chile bean paste, to taste

1–2 tsp chile oil, to taste

2 tsp sesame oil

2 tsp neutral cooking oil

I make these spicy noodles when I need something to awaken my taste buds. You can tailor the heat level by adjusting the amount of chile oil and bean paste, adding less for a milder version. *Pictured overleaf, top right.*

Bring a large pot of water to a boil. Add the noodles and cook according to the package instructions. Drain, then leave to steam-dry in the colander.

In a small bowl, mix together the remaining ingredients, except the cooking oil, saving some of the scallion greens for the garnish.

Heat the cooking oil in a large wok or frying pan over high heat. Add the noodles and stir-fry for 2–3 minutes until they are getting crispy. Add the sauce around the edges of the pan and toss to combine. Cook for 1–2 minutes until the noodles have absorbed the sauce. Adjust the seasonings.

Serve, garnished with the reserved scallion greens.

清汤面
4. Simple Soup Noodles VE

Ingredients

2 servings of noodles (any kind)

9 oz (250 g) bok choi (or any other leafy green)

2 tsp neutral cooking oil

1 small piece of fresh ginger root, peeled and minced

1 garlic clove, minced

2 scallions, finely chopped (white and green parts separated)

2 tsp light soy sauce

2 tsp mushroom stir-fry sauce

1 tsp sesame oil

3 cups (700 ml) boiling water or stock (any kind)

This is a super-quick base recipe for when you want a warming bowl of noodle soup in less than 10 minutes. The variations are endless.

Bring a large pot of water to a boil. Add the noodles and cook according to the package instructions. In the last 2–3 minutes of cooking time, add the bok choi to the pot. Drain, then set aside.

Heat the oil in a small pan over high heat.

Divide the ginger, garlic and scallion whites evenly between two bowls. Pour the hot oil evenly over the bowls. Divide the light soy sauce, mushroom stir-fry sauce and sesame oil evenly between the bowls. Top up with boiling hot water or stock.

Transfer the cooked noodles to the bowls, garnish with the scallion greens and serve.

酸辣面
5. Hot and Sour Soup Noodles VE

Ingredients

2 servings thick vermicelli noodles (or any noodle)

4 tsp neutral cooking oil

1 small piece of fresh ginger root, peeled and minced

1 garlic clove, minced

2 tsp chile bean paste

2 scallions, finely chopped (white and green parts separated)

2 tbsp black rice vinegar

1–2 tsp chile oil, or more to taste

1 tbsp light soy sauce

1 tbsp sesame oil

pinch of ground Sichuan peppercorns (optional)

3 cups (700 ml) boiling water or stock (any kind)

This recipe is inspired by one of my favorite Sichuan dishes, *suan la fen* 酸辣粉, or hot and sour noodle soup. It's a spicy and tangy soup served with thick vermicelli noodles. You can compose the dish directly in the serving bowls and top up with cooked vegetables and protein of your choice. *Pictured on page 97, bottom right.*

Bring a large pot of water to a boil. Add the noodles and cook according to the package instructions. Drain and set aside.

Heat the oil in a small pan over high heat.

Divide the ginger, garlic, chile bean paste and scallion whites evenly between two serving bowls. Pour the hot oil evenly over the bowls. Divide the black rice vinegar, chile oil, light soy sauce, sesame oil and Sichuan pepper (if using) evenly between the bowls. Top up with boiling water or stock.

Transfer the cooked noodles to the bowls, garnish with the scallion greens and serve.

chapter

easy weekend winners

three

Serves 4–6

白切鸡

White-Cut Chicken with Ginger and Scallion Sauce

There is one dish that's served at almost every one of our family gatherings—and that's my grandmother's steamed chicken. The name "white-cut" refers to how the chicken retains its light color after cooking since it's either steamed or poached. My grandmother prefers steaming because it brings out more chicken flavor. She also adds more seasoning in the marinade to ensure a golden yellow color. She always uses the nicest chicken she can find in the market, so a high-quality organic or free-range chicken makes a big difference.

Time

1 hour–1 hour 10 minutes, plus overnight marinating

Ingredients

1 large whole chicken (free-range and organic is best), oven-ready

1 large piece of fresh ginger root, peeled and thinly sliced into discs

2 tbsp sesame oil

1 serving of Ginger and Scallion Sauce (page 187)

For the marinade

2 tsp sugar

1½ tbsp salt

2 tbsp water

2 tbsp Shaoxing rice wine

1 tbsp light soy sauce

2 tsp dark soy sauce

In a small bowl, mix the marinade ingredients together. Place the chicken in a large bowl or container, pour the marinade over the chicken and massage for 2–3 minutes until evenly distributed. Cover with plastic wrap and leave to marinate in the fridge overnight.

Remove the chicken from the fridge and place breast-side down in a large heatproof dish. Stuff the ginger slices into the cavity.

Prepare a steamer large enough to hold the whole chicken (see pages 20–1). Place the dish with the chicken inside. Steam over medium heat for 15 minutes, then flip the chicken breast-side up. Steam for a further 25–30 minutes until cooked through.

Remove from the steamer and, while the chicken is still hot, brush all over with the sesame oil. Leave to rest for 10–15 minutes.

Cut the chicken into smaller pieces and place on a large platter. Pour over some of the chicken steaming juices and serve with the ginger and scallion sauce.

Note

This dish is similar to another popular chicken dish, Hainanese Chicken. However, Hainanese Chicken is usually served with seasoned rice, a bowl of soup and a variety of dipping sauces. The chicken is also blanched in iced water after cooking to give the chicken skin a better texture. White-Cut Chicken is poached or steamed and simply served with the ginger and scallion sauce.

Serves 4

红烧肉
Red Braised Pork Belly

Time
1¼–1½ hours

Ingredients

1 large piece of fresh ginger root, peeled and thinly sliced into discs

3 scallions, cut into thirds

1 lb (500 g) skin-on pork belly, sliced into 1 in (3 cm) chunks

1 tbsp neutral cooking oil

1 oz (35 g) rock sugar (or 3 tbsp regular sugar) (see Note)

2 bay leaves

2 star anise

1½ tbsp light soy sauce

1 tbsp dark soy sauce

1 tbsp Shaoxing rice wine

1 x 15 oz (440 ml) can of light beer

salt, to taste

Red-braising is a Chinese method of slow-cooking with soy sauce that gives the final dish a slightly red hue. The history of this dish isn't clear, but one theory is that hundreds of years ago a man was playing chess and accidentally cooked his pork belly for too long, creating that famous thick glossy sauce and melt-in-your-mouth tender pork. It's an easy, classic Chinese dish that you really must give a try.

Bring a large pot filled with water to a boil, add half of the ginger, half of the scallions, a pinch of salt and the pork belly. Boil for 2–3 minutes, then drain (any foam should have risen to the top and the inside of the pork should still be pink, see Note). Set aside.

Heat the oil in a large wok or pan that has a lid over medium-low heat. Add the blanched pork and stir-fry for 10–15 minutes until most of the fat has rendered. Use a slotted spoon to transfer the pork to a plate. Pour the pork fat into a small bowl and set aside.

Heat 1 tablespoon of the pork fat in the same pan over medium heat. Add the sugar and cook for 3–5 minutes until the sugar has melted and turned lightly golden. Return the pork to the pan and cook for 2–3 minutes, stirring until the pork is coated in the sugar. Add the remaining ingredients and bring to a boil. Cover with the lid, then reduce the heat to low and simmer for 45 minutes–1 hour, stirring occasionally, until the sauce has reduced and thickened.

Taste to adjust the seasoning. Transfer to a serving dish and serve with rice.

Notes

Blanching meat is a common Chinese cooking technique used to remove the impurities in meat, such as blood and dirt. Proteins like pork or beef are placed in cold water, then brought to a boil, or cooked in boiling water for several minutes then drained. The Chinese believe that this gives the meat a nicer texture and a cleaner flavor.

Rock sugar is a type of sugar composed of large sugar crystals. It's often used in Chinese cooking, and throughout Asia, because it lends a milder sweetness than regular white sugar. It's also often used in Chinese desserts because it adds a light brown color. A substitute for rock sugar is either white sugar or light brown sugar.

干烧伊面
Longevity Noodles VG

Serves 4

This dish is made with a special type of noodle called *yi mien* 伊麵. The noodles are fried, then packaged and sold in large, round, golden bricks. They're hard to miss in the noodle aisle. These long chewy noodles are often served during Lunar New Year or on birthdays, because their long shape represents long life. If you can't find these specific noodles, other medium-thickness noodles will work too.

Time

20 minutes

Ingredients

2 bundles of longevity noodles (or 4 servings of medium-thickness wheat noodles)

1 tbsp neutral cooking oil

4 scallions, cut into thirds

4–6 dried shiitake mushrooms, rehydrated (reserving the soaking liquid, if wished, see below) and thinly sliced

9 oz (250 g) bok choi, thinly sliced

For the sauce

1 tbsp mushroom stir-fry sauce

1 tbsp light soy sauce

1 tsp dark soy sauce

2 tsp sesame oil

½ tsp salt

1 tsp sugar

pinch of ground white pepper

1¼ cups (300 ml) vegetable stock (or mushroom soaking liquid)

For the cornstarch slurry

1 tbsp cornstarch

3 tbsp water

Bring a large pot of water to a boil, add the noodles and cook for 4–5 minutes until soft with a slight bite. (If using other types of noodles, cook according to the package instructions.) Drain, then rinse under cold water and set aside.

In a large jug or bowl, mix together the ingredients for the sauce.

Heat the oil in a large wok or pan over high heat. Add the scallions and cook for 2–3 minutes until fragrant. Add the mushrooms and mix to combine, then add the bok choi and the sauce and bring to a boil. Taste to adjust the seasonings.

In a small bowl, mix together the ingredients for the cornstarch slurry, then slowly pour the slurry into the main pan while continuously stirring. Boil for 1–2 minutes until thickened.

Add the noodles and cook for a final 3–4 minutes, or until most of the sauce has been absorbed.

Transfer to a large plate and serve.

烤豬腩肉

Grandma's Boozy Pork Belly

Time

15–20 minutes, plus 1 hour or overnight marinating

Ingredients

1 lb (500 g) pork belly (or 1 lb 8 oz/700 g pork ribs), cut into 2 in (5 cm) long pieces

1 tbsp light soy sauce

3 tbsp Shaoxing rice wine

2 tbsp water

1 tsp sesame oil

2 tsp cornstarch

1 tsp sugar

1 tsp salt

½ tsp ground white pepper

1 tbsp neutral cooking oil

Whenever I go to my grandma's house for lunch, she often whips up this delicious baked pork. Sometimes she uses pork ribs, other times she opts for pork belly, my grandpa's favorite cut of meat. The secret to her recipe is adding quite a significant amount of Chinese cooking wine to not only flavor the meat but to tenderize it, too. She bakes the pork belly in her tiny countertop toaster oven, but I think it would also work really well stir-fried.

Place the pork in a large bowl and add all the remaining ingredients, except the cooking oil. Massage for 2–3 minutes, then leave in the fridge to marinate for at least 1 hour, or overnight.

Preheat the oven to 350°F (180°C).

Place the pork on a baking sheet lined with parchment paper and drizzle with the cooking oil. Bake for 15–20 minutes until cooked all the way through and golden brown.

Transfer to a large platter and serve.

Serves 2–4*

蒸魚
Simple Steamed Fish PESC

Hong Kongers take their steamed fish very seriously. My uncles and aunts argue over the perfect amount of time to steam a whole fish. Depending on the type of fish, we believe there are different preparations to bring out each variety's natural flavors. Some fish should be steamed with dried tangerine peel, others with fermented soybeans, and so on. This recipe is the most simple, all-purpose method to steam any kind of fish. Ask anyone, one of the best parts of a steamed fish is the sauce—I always enjoy my steamed fish with rice to soak it all up.

Time

15–20 minutes, depending on size and type of fish

Ingredients

1 whole fish, de-scaled, fins trimmed, gutted and thoroughly cleaned (or 4 fish fillets, any kind) (see Note)

1 large piece of fresh ginger root, peeled and half julienned; half thinly sliced into discs

2 tbsp neutral cooking oil

5 scallions, julienned

1 large handful of fresh cilantro, roughly torn

1 large red chile, thinly sliced (optional)

For the sauce

1 tbsp light soy sauce

1 tsp dark soy sauce

1 tsp sugar

¼ tsp ground white pepper

1 tsp Shaoxing rice wine (optional)

If using a whole fish, place the fish on a heatproof plate and stuff the cavity with the ginger discs. If using fish fillets, place the ginger underneath and on top of the fillets.

Prepare a steamer large enough to hold the whole fish or fillets (see pages 20-1). Place the dish with the fish inside.

Steam over medium heat for 10–12 minutes, depending on the size of the fish. When the fish is almost fully cooked, turn the heat off and leave the fish to cook in the leftover steam for 2–3 minutes. Use a butter knife to test whether the meat is tender and opaque. Be careful not to overcook the fish (see Note).

If using fish fillets, reduce the steaming time to 6–8 minutes, then test for doneness (see Note).

Meanwhile, in a small bowl, mix together the ingredients for the sauce. Taste to adjust the seasoning.

When the fish is done, drain most of the fish steaming juices from the plate. Heat the oil in a small pan over high heat.

Place the scallions, julienned ginger and cilantro on top of the cooked fish. Pour over the hot oil (the ingredients should sizzle immediately), then pour over the sauce and garnish with sliced chile (if using). Serve straight to the table.

Notes

*Depending on size of the fish.

In Hong Kong, we usually only steam white fish, such as grouper, sea bream, pomfret, etc. My family buys fish according to what's in season and sold in the markets. Ask your local fishmonger what's the best fish of the season. My dad's trick for finding fresh fish is to look for clear, bright eyes.

The thickness of your fish will affect the cooking time. Fish around 1½–2 in (4–5 cm) thick can take up to 15 minutes to fully cook. Fish around ¾–1 in (2–3 cm) thick could be done in less than 10 minutes. I check for doneness after 6–8 minutes. If the fish feels almost cooked but not quite, turn the heat off and leave to cook in the leftover steam for up to 3 minutes.

Serves 4

焗豬扒饭
Baked Tomato Pork Chop with Fried Rice

Time
30–40 minutes, plus marinating

Ingredients
4 pork chops
neutral cooking oil
5¼ oz (150 g) firm mozzarella, grated

For the marinade
1 egg
1 tbsp light soy sauce
2 tsp cornstarch
1 tsp ground white pepper
1 tsp salt
½ tsp sugar

For the rice
2 eggs
4 servings of cooked and cooled jasmine rice (3¾ cups/600 g cooked from 1¼ cups/240 g uncooked rice, see page 18)
1 tsp salt
½ tsp sugar
pinch of ground white pepper

For the sauce
1 onion, cut into ¾ in (2 cm) chunks
7 oz (200 g) canned pineapple slices, drained and cut into ¾ in (2 cm) chunks
2 large tomatoes, diced
6 tbsp ketchup
4 tbsp tomato paste
1 tsp light soy sauce
½ tsp salt
½ tsp sugar
1 cup (250 ml) water, or as needed, plus 3½ tbsp for the cornstarch slurry
1 tbsp cornstarch

There are many local chain restaurants in Hong Kong famous for serving this dish. If you ever walk in during a busy lunch hour, you'll see many people eating it as a set lunch. Essentially, it's fried rice topped with a pork chop and covered with tomato sauce and cheese. It's one of the most famous dishes in "Soy Sauce Western Cuisine," a style of food that emerged during Hong Kong's British colonial rule, which combines Western and Chinese cooking.

Place the pork in a large bowl with all the marinade ingredients. Massage for 2–3 minutes until well combined. Leave to marinate for at least 20 minutes, or overnight in the fridge.

Preheat the oven to 400°F (200°C).

For the rice, heat 2 teaspoons of cooking oil in a wok or large pan over high heat. Crack in the eggs and scramble for 2–3 minutes until just cooked. Push the egg to the back of the pan and add the rice. Cook for 3–5 minutes, breaking up any clumps with the back of the spatula. Toss vigorously with the egg to combine. Season with the salt, sugar and white pepper, then taste to adjust. Transfer to a large baking dish.

Reheat the same pan over medium heat and add 1 tablespoon of cooking oil. Add the marinated pork and cook for 6–8 minutes, turning halfway, until golden brown and cooked through. Place the cooked pork chops on top of the rice in the baking dish.

For the sauce, add 2 teaspoons of cooking oil to the same pan and set over high heat. Add the onion and cook for 2–3 minutes until lightly charred. Add the pineapple and tomatoes, and cook for 2–3 minutes, then add the remaining sauce ingredients, except the cornstarch, and bring to a boil. Cook for 3–4 minutes, adding more water if you want a thinner sauce.

In a small bowl, mix the cornstarch with 3 tablespoons of water to make a slurry. Reduce the heat to low, then slowly pour the mixture into the sauce while continuously stirring. Cook for 1–2 minutes until thickened. Taste to adjust the seasonings.

Pour the sauce over the pork chops and rice, and sprinkle over the cheese. Transfer to the oven and bake for 6–8 minutes until the cheese is melted and deep golden brown.

Serve straight to the table.

Serves 4

港式魚香茄子煲
Cantonese-Style Clay Pot Eggplant VE

Time
20 minutes

Ingredients

2 eggplants, sliced into thick batons

1 tbsp distilled white vinegar (or any light-colored vinegar, see note)

1 tbsp neutral cooking oil

3 garlic cloves, crushed

1 large piece of fresh ginger root, peeled and sliced into thin discs

3 scallions, sliced into thirds

2–3 tsp chile bean paste, to taste

For the sauce

1 tbsp Shaoxing rice wine

1 tbsp black rice vinegar

1 tsp mushroom stir-fry sauce

1 tsp dark soy sauce

2 tsp light soy sauce

½ tsp sugar

pinch of ground white pepper

⅔ cup (150 ml) water or stock (any kind)

Hong Kongers are not known for having a high spice tolerance. This recipe is a simpler and less spicy version of *yu xiang qie zi* 魚香茄子, a famous sweet, sour and spicy eggplant dish from Sichuan. Many home cooks like to prepare the dish in a wok or pan, then transfer to a heated clay pot or lidded Dutch oven to keep the dish warm as it's served.

Place the eggplant in a large bowl and cover with cold water. Add the vinegar and mix. Set aside while you prepare the rest of your ingredients.

In a small bowl, mix together the ingredients for the sauce. Set aside.

Prepare a steamer large enough to hold the eggplant (see pages 20–1). Drain the eggplant, place in the steamer and steam for 5 minutes, or until tender and a fork easily runs through the flesh.

Heat the oil in a large wok or pot over high heat. Add the garlic, ginger and most of the scallions (save some, thinly sliced, for garnish) and cook for 2–3 minutes until fragrant. Add the chile bean paste and cook for 2–3 minutes until sizzling. Add the sauce around the edges of the pan and bring to a boil, then add the steamed eggplants and gently stir to combine. Cook for 4–5 minutes, or until the eggplant has absorbed most of the sauce. If you want a drier sauce, continue cooking until most of the sauce has evaporated.

Serve on a large plate and garnish with the reserved scallions.

Note
Steaming the eggplant gives it a juicy and meaty texture, as well as a brighter purple color. The vinegar removes any bitterness from the eggplant and gives it a slight bite, as opposed to salting the eggplant, which turns it slightly mushy. You can use any light- or clear-colored vinegar here, such as rice vinegar, apple cider vinegar or white wine vinegar.

Serves 2

锅烧豆腐
Crispy Tofu with Spicy Mushroom Gravy ^{VG}

Time
20 minutes

Ingredients

1 tsp neutral cooking oil

1–2 tsp chile bean paste

2 garlic cloves, finely chopped

1 small piece of fresh ginger root, peeled and finely chopped

2 scallions, thinly sliced (white and green parts separated)

4–6 dried shiitake mushrooms, rehydrated (reserving the soaking liquid, if you wish, see below) and finely chopped (or use fresh mushrooms)

For the crispy tofu

1 egg, beaten

⅔ cup (70 g) cornstarch

salt and ground white pepper

1 tbsp neutral cooking oil

1 x 14 oz (400 g) block of medium-firm tofu, cut into ½ in (1 cm) thick rectangles

For the sauce

scant 1 cup (200 ml) mushroom soaking liquid, water or stock (any kind)

1 tbsp Shaoxing rice wine

1 tsp light soy sauce

1½ tsp mushroom stir-fry sauce

1 tsp dark soy sauce

1 tsp sesame oil

2 tsp cornstarch

2 tbsp water

Tofu is a traditional ingredient that has been consumed in China for over 2,000 years. It's often served alongside meat and seafood dishes, and is not seen as a meat alternative. Here, crispy bites of tofu are smothered in a delicious, spicy mushroom sauce. For a non-spicy version, feel free to skip the chile bean paste. If cooking for a crowd, you can make the sauce ahead of time and keep the tofu crispy and warm in the oven.

For the crispy tofu, crack the egg into a bowl and whisk until smooth. Place the cornstarch in another bowl and season with salt and white pepper.

Heat the oil in a wok or frying pan over medium-high heat. Coat the tofu in the egg, then coat in the cornstarch. Shake off any excess, then gently place the tofu into the hot oil. Cook for 3–4 minutes on each side until golden brown. Transfer to a serving plate and set aside.

In a small bowl, mix together the ingredients for the sauce.

Reheat the pan over high heat with the teaspoon of cooking oil. Add the chile bean paste and cook for 1–2 minutes until sizzling. Add the garlic, ginger and scallion whites, and cook for 1–2 minutes until fragrant. Add the mushrooms and mix to combine. Add the sauce around the edges of the pan and bring to a boil. Cook for 2–3 minutes until the sauce thickens. Taste to adjust the seasonings.

Pour the mixture over the tofu, garnish with the scallion greens and serve.

Serves 4

福建炒饭
Fujian Fried Rice

Sometimes called Hokkien fried rice, this popular dish consists of simple egg fried rice served with a glorious meat and seafood gravy. I've used a mixture of chicken and shrimp, but you can also use pork, or just shrimp to make it pescatarian, or firm tofu for vegetarians. You can also use other vegetables, just make sure they are chopped up small so they mix well with the rice.

Time
20–25 minutes

Ingredients

2 tsp neutral cooking oil

1 carrot, cut into ½ in (1 cm) cubes

1 small piece of fresh ginger root, peeled and finely chopped

2 scallions, thinly sliced (white and green parts separated)

3 garlic cloves, finely chopped

1 chicken breast, cut into small cubes

3 oz (80 g) raw shelled shrimp, deveined, cut into ¾ in (2 cm) pieces

3 oz (80 g) asparagus, cut into ½ in (1 cm) pieces

For the rice

2 tsp neutral cooking oil

2 eggs

4 servings of cooked and cooled jasmine rice (3¾ cups/600 g cooked from 1¼ cups/240 g uncooked rice, see page 18)

½ tsp salt

¼ tsp ground white pepper

For the sauce

1¼ cups (300 ml) water or stock

1 tbsp oyster sauce

1 tsp sesame oil

½ tsp sugar

½ tsp salt

¼ tsp ground white pepper

For the cornstarch slurry

2 tsp cornstarch

2 tbsp water

For the rice, heat the oil in a wok or large pot over high heat. Crack in the egg and scramble for 1–2 minutes, running a spatula across the egg. Add the rice and spread it out into an even layer. Leave to cook for 1–2 minutes undisturbed. Breaking up any clumps with the back of the spatula, cook for a further 3–5 minutes, tossing vigorously to combine. Season with salt and white pepper. Transfer to a large serving platter and set aside.

In a small bowl, mix together the ingredients for the sauce. In a separate bowl, mix together the ingredients for the cornstarch slurry.

Add the 2 teaspoons of oil to the same pan and set over high heat. Add the carrot and cook for 2–3 minutes until softening. Add the ginger, scallion whites and garlic, and cook for 1–2 minutes until fragrant. Add the sauce around the edges of the pan, bring to a boil then reduce the heat to low. Add the chicken and shrimp and simmer for 3–5 minutes until almost cooked through. Add the asparagus and cook for 1–2 minutes until softened.

Reduce the heat to low then add the cornstarch slurry while continuously stirring. Bring to a boil and cook for 1–2 minutes until thickened. Taste to adjust the seasonings.

Pour the sauce over the fried rice, garnish with scallion greens and serve.

Serves 4

避風塘炒虾

Typhoon Shelter Shrimp PESC

Time
20–25 minutes

Ingredients

<u>For the shrimp</u>

14 oz (400 g) raw shelled shrimp, deveined (see Note if using shell-on shrimp)

3 tbsp cornstarch

salt and ground white pepper, to taste

1 tbsp neutral cooking oil

<u>For the coating</u>

3 tbsp neutral cooking oil

1 whole bulb of garlic, cloves finely chopped

2/3 cup (30 g) panko breadcrumbs

1 large piece of fresh ginger root, peeled and finely chopped

3 scallions, finely chopped (white and green parts separated)

1–2 large red chiles, thinly sliced (deseeded for less heat, if you wish)

1/2 tsp sugar

salt and ground white pepper

This dish is traditionally prepared with crab and was created in the 1960s on fishing boats located in Hong Kong's typhoon shelters. These shelters were constructed as a place for fishermen to hide out during the city's many tropical rainstorms. Nowadays, many seafood restaurants serve this dish featuring a very generous amount of garlic and at varying levels of spiciness. It's one of my favorite dishes and it's hard to find outside of Hong Kong.

Pat the shrimp dry, place in a bowl and coat with the cornstarch. Season with salt and white pepper.

Heat the oil in a large wok or pot over medium-high heat. Add the shrimp and cook for 4–6 minutes, turning halfway, until golden and almost cooked through. Transfer to a plate and set aside while you make the coating.

To the same pan, add the oil and set over medium-low heat. Add the garlic and cook for 6–8 minutes until very light golden brown (be careful not to burn it). Strain out the garlic through a fine-mesh sieve into a bowl, reserving the garlic oil and setting the fried garlic aside.

Return the garlic oil to the pan. Add the breadcrumbs and cook over medium heat for 3–4 minutes until light golden brown. Add the ginger, scallion whites and chiles, and cook for 2–3 minutes until fragrant. Return the fried garlic and shrimp to the pan. Cook for 2–3 minutes, tossing to combine. Season with the sugar, salt and white pepper, and taste to adjust.

Transfer to a large serving platter and garnish with the remaining scallion greens, if liked.

<u>Note</u>

If using shell-on shrimp, follow the same method but cook the shrimp for 6–8 minutes until almost cooked through. Do not overcook the shrimp in the first step because they will cook again with the rest of the ingredients.

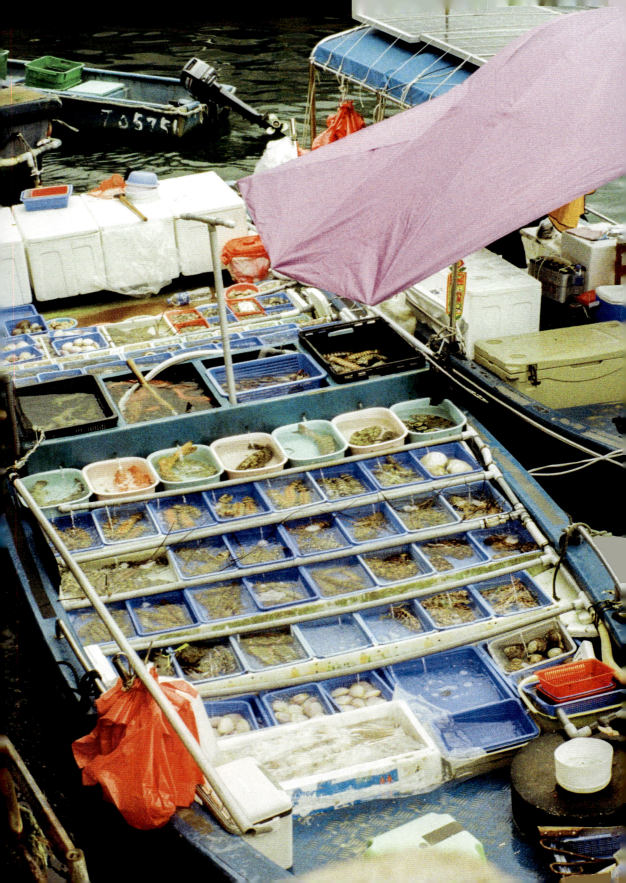

Serves 4–6

蚝油焖冬菇

Whole Braised Mushrooms VE

Time

20–25 minutes (or up to 1 hour)

Ingredients

1 lb 12 oz (800 g) baby bok choi, cut in half lengthways (or broccoli florets)

For the braised mushrooms

2 tsp neutral cooking oil

1 small piece of fresh ginger root, peeled and finely chopped

2 garlic cloves, finely chopped

12 dried shiitake mushrooms, rehydrated (reserving the soaking liquid, if wished, see below)

generous 2 cups (500 ml) mushroom soaking liquid, water or stock (any kind)

1 tsp mushroom-stir fry sauce

1 tsp light soy sauce

½ tsp dark soy sauce

½ tsp sugar

salt and ground white pepper, to taste

For the cornstarch slurry

1 tbsp cornstarch

3½ tbsp water

In Chinese culture, mushrooms symbolize health and longevity. For that reason, they are always served at Lunar New Year feasts. My grandmother makes a variety of braised mushroom dishes, sometimes braising them for over 6 hours so the mushrooms absorb maximum flavor. Dried shiitake mushrooms are essential to this dish.

Heat the oil in a wok or large sauté pan over medium heat. Add the ginger and garlic, and cook for 1–2 minutes until fragrant. Add the mushrooms and toss to combine, then add the remaining braised mushroom ingredients. Bring to a boil, then reduce the heat to low and simmer for 10–15 minutes (or up to 1 hour, topping up with water when necessary) until the mushrooms have absorbed some of the sauce. Taste to adjust the seasonings.

In a small bowl, mix together the ingredients for the cornstarch slurry.

In the last 5 minutes of cooking the mushrooms, bring a large pot of water to a boil. Add the bok choi and cook for 2–3 minutes until soft. Drain, then transfer to a serving platter. (Optional: arrange the bok choi in a circle around the outer edges of the plate, for a traditional way of serving.)

Remove the mushrooms from the sauce and place in the middle of the serving platter.

Reduce the heat under the sauce to low. Slowly pour in the cornstarch slurry, while continuously stirring, and bring to a boil. Cook for 1–2 minutes until thickened, then taste to adjust the seasoning. Pour the sauce over the mushrooms and serve.

Note

Dotted around Hong Kong are shops selling dried goods like dried fruit, herbs, nuts, etc. In these shops you'll find large glass jars filled with mushrooms of all sizes, from the size of a nickel to mushrooms larger than the palm of your hand. For Lunar New Year, my grandmother always bought the largest and nicest mushrooms she could find, but you can use any grade of whole dried mushrooms available to you.

鮮蝦粉絲煲
Shrimp Clay Pot Vermicelli PESC

Time
30–35 minutes

Ingredients
7 oz (200 g) vermicelli noodles

2 shallots, thinly sliced

4 scallions, cut into thirds

1 large piece of fresh ginger root, peeled and finely chopped

5 garlic cloves, finely chopped

small handful of fresh cilantro

For the sauce
2½ cups (600 ml) water or stock (any kind)

2 tbsp Shaoxing rice wine

2 tsp light soy sauce

2 tsp dark soy sauce

2 tsp oyster sauce

2 tsp sesame oil

½ tsp sugar

salt and ground white pepper, to taste

For the shrimp option
7 oz (200 g) raw shelled shrimp (see Note)

salt and ground white pepper

2 tbsp neutral cooking oil

For the vegetarian option
2 tsp neutral cooking oil

1 x 14 oz (400 g) block of medium-firm tofu, cut into ½ in (1 cm) thick rectangles

1 tsp light soy sauce

1 tsp mushroom-stir fry sauce

1 tsp dark soy sauce

1 tsp sesame oil

Hong Kongers love seafood. Apart from steamed fish, shrimp are always part of the Lunar New Year feast. Here, vermicelli noodles soak up all the delicious shrimp flavors. Despite the name, you don't have to cook it in a clay pot; you can use a Dutch oven instead.

Place the noodles in a large bowl, cover with cold water and soak for 10 minutes. Mix together all the ingredients for the sauce in a large bowl and set aside.

For the shrimp version: Pat the shrimp dry and season with salt and white pepper. Heat the oil in a deep pan or Dutch oven (with a tight-fitting lid) over high heat. Add the shrimp and cook for 6–8 minutes until almost cooked through. Use a slotted spoon to scoop the shrimp out of the oil onto a plate and set aside.

For the vegetarian version: Heat the oil in a deep pan or Dutch oven over medium heat. Add the tofu and cook for 6–8 minutes, turning halfway, until golden brown. Add the remaining ingredients and turn to coat. Adjust the seasonings, transfer to a plate and set aside.

For both versions: Reheat the same oil in the pan over medium-high heat. Add the shallots and cook for 3–5 minutes until softened.

Add most of the scallions (save some, thinly sliced, for garnish) along with the ginger and garlic, and cook for 2–3 minutes until fragrant. Add 1⅔ cups (400 ml) of the sauce and the drained noodles, and mix to combine. Cover the pan with the lid and cook for 4–6 minutes until the noodles are cooked through and have absorbed almost all of the sauce. If it starts to dry out before the noodles are fully cooked, add more sauce as needed.

<u>If making the shrimp version:</u> Return the shrimp to the pan and cook for 1–2 minutes until the noodles have absorbed all of the sauce and the shrimp are hot. Taste to adjust the seasonings. Serve garnished with the cilantro and reserved sliced scallions.

<u>If making the vegetarian version:</u> Continue to cook the noodles until they have absorbed all of the sauce. Taste to adjust the seasonings. Top the noodles with the tofu and serve garnished with the cilantro and reserved sliced scallions.

Note
This dish is usually made with shell-on shrimp. The shells add extra flavor to the dish, especially as the noodles absorb all the sauce. However, I opt for shelled shrimp for ease. If you would prefer to use shell-on shrimp, cook the shrimp for 8–10 minutes until almost cooked through, then proceed with the recipe as stated.

糖醋小排
Sweet and Sour Pork Ribs

Time
50–55 minutes

Ingredients
1 lb 8 oz (700 g) pork ribs

1 tsp baking soda

1 tbsp neutral cooking oil

3 oz (80 g) rock sugar (or white sugar, or light brown sugar)

1 large piece of fresh ginger root, peeled and sliced into thin discs

4 scallions, trimmed and halved

2 star anise

2 tbsp light soy sauce

1 tbsp dark soy sauce

3 tbsp black rice vinegar

1 tsp salt

generous 2 cups (500 ml) water or stock (any kind)

1 tsp sesame seeds, to garnish

This dish looks impressive, but it's one of the easiest recipes in the book. No marinating. No blanching. Just simmering on the stovetop while you go about the rest of your day. I know it seems odd to add so much sugar to a meat dish, but the Shanghainese are famous for balancing sweet and salty flavors. Depending on your taste, you might want a sweeter or tangier sauce, so the amount of sugar and vinegar you add is up to you.

Place the ribs in a large mixing bowl, add the baking soda and a small splash of water and massage for 2–3 minutes. Transfer the ribs to a large tray, letting the excess water drain off, and pat dry with paper towels.

Heat the oil in a large wok or pot over medium-high heat. Add the ribs and cook for 5–7 minutes, turning occasionally, until golden brown. Add the sugar and cook for 2–3 minutes until melted. Add the ginger, scallions and star anise, mix to combine and cook for 1–2 minutes until fragrant. Add the light and dark soy sauces, 2 tablespoons of the black rice vinegar, salt and water or stock.

Bring to a boil, then cover with a lid and reduce to a simmer. Cook for 30–35 minutes until most of the liquid has evaporated and the sauce has turned into a glaze.

Remove the lid and add the remaining tablespoon of black rice vinegar. Taste to adjust the seasonings. If the sauce is still quite thin, remove the lid and cook for a further 3–4 minutes until the sauce turns into a runny glaze and coats the ribs.

Transfer to a large serving platter and garnish with the sesame seeds.

Note
I add black rice vinegar twice during the cooking process because, as the vinegar cooks, the acidic flavor fades. Adding more vinegar at the end brings back some fresh acidity to the dish.

烤豉油鸡
Baked Whole Soy Sauce Chicken

Time
1 hour 25 minutes, plus 1 hour or overnight marinating

Ingredients
1 large whole chicken (free-range or organic is best)

1 tbsp salt

For the sauce
1 tbsp neutral cooking oil

2 shallots, quartered

1 large piece of fresh ginger root, peeled and thinly sliced into discs

3 garlic cloves, crushed

3 scallions, cut into thirds

4 tbsp light soy sauce

3 tbsp dark soy sauce

1½ oz (40 g) rock sugar (or light brown sugar)

There are dozens of ways to cook soy sauce chicken. Some people poach the chicken in a soy sauce broth. Others place it in the rice cooker and let the machine do the work. In my recipe, I salt the chicken ahead of time to make it unbelievably tender, then baste it in a delicious soy sauce marinade and bake until deeply golden brown and crispy. So simple, yet so tasty.

Place the chicken into a large container and rub with the salt. Place in the fridge and leave to marinate for at least 1 hour, or overnight for best results.

For the sauce, heat the oil in a small saucepan over high heat. Add the shallots, ginger, garlic and scallions, and cook for 3–4 minutes until fragrant. Add the light soy sauce, dark soy sauce and sugar, reduce the heat to low and simmer for 3–4 minutes until the sugar has dissolved.

Preheat the oven to 350°F (180°C).

Place the chicken onto a wire rack with a roasting pan underneath to catch the juices, and brush the chicken all over with one-third of the sauce. Bake for 25 minutes.

Remove the chicken from the oven and brush with more sauce. Return to the oven to bake for another 25 minutes.

Remove from the oven and increase the oven temperature to 400°F (200°C). Brush the chicken with more sauce, then bake for another 10–12 minutes until golden brown and cooked through. Depending on the size of your chicken, cooking times may vary. Soy sauce tends to burn easily, so keep an eye on the chicken to prevent the skin from burning.

Remove from the oven and leave the chicken to rest for at least 15 minutes.

Carve the chicken into smaller pieces, then transfer to a large serving platter and pour over the chicken roasting juices.

Note
If you like, you can make a gravy to go with the chicken. Combine any leftover sauce and the chicken roasting juices in a small saucepan. Bring to a boil, then reduce the heat to low. In a small bowl, make a cornstarch slurry by mixing 2 teaspoons cornstarch with 2 tablespoons water. Slowly pour the cornstarch slurry into the gravy, while continuously stirring. Boil for 1–2 minutes until thickened. Taste to adjust the seasoning.

Serves 4

叉燒
Char Siu

Time
1 hour, plus 1 hour or overnight marinating

Ingredients
1 lb 5 oz (600 g) pork shoulder, cut into long strips, 1 in (3 cm) wide (see Note)

4 tbsp Sweetened Soy Sauce (see page 191), to serve (optional)

For the sauce
4½ tbsp light brown sugar

3 tbsp Shaoxing rice wine

3 tbsp hoisin sauce

3 tbsp oyster sauce (or mushroom stir-fry sauce)

1 tbsp light soy sauce

1 tsp Chinese five spice

½ tsp ground white pepper

1½ tsp salt

1 tsp garlic powder (optional)

3 tbsp honey

Notes
When making char siu at home, try to find pork shoulder that has a nice amount of fat to help the pork stay juicy during the long cooking time. If your pork comes in 1–2 large pieces, cut the pieces in half lengthways so you get several long, thin pieces of meat rather than one large piece of roast pork. This way, each piece gets coated in more sauce.

Char siu is one of the easiest Hong Kong roast meat dishes to make at home. Most restaurants add red food coloring to make it look more appealing. Homemade versions will have a darker brown color, but are equally, if not more, delicious. The method may look long, but it's actually very simple and mostly hands-off.

Place the pork on a chopping board and poke holes in it with a fork. This will tenderize the meat and help it absorb the marinade. In a jug or bowl, mix together the ingredients for the sauce, leaving out the honey for later.

Place the pork in a large bowl or sealable plastic bag and pour in the sauce, reserving around ⅓ cup (80 ml) for basting. Place in the fridge to marinate for at least 1 hour, or ideally overnight.

Add the honey to the reserved sauce and mix to combine.

<u>To roast:</u> Preheat the oven to 475°F (245°C). Line a large roasting pan with aluminum foil.

Place the pork on a metal rack over the pan. Pour ⅔ cup (150 ml) water into the bottom of the pan to prevent the juices from burning. Baste the pork with 2–3 tablespoons of the sauce. Roast for 10 minutes.

Remove the pork from the oven and baste with 2–3 tablespoons of the sauce. Reduce the oven temperature to 375°F (190°C). Return the pork to the oven and roast for 15 minutes.

Remove from the oven, flip the pork and baste with 2–3 tablespoons of the sauce. If the juices start to stick, add a splash of water to prevent burning. Roast for 15 minutes.

Remove from the oven. Turn on the broiler to high heat. Baste the pork with the remaining sauce and the cooking juices from the pan. Broil for 5–10 minutes until golden brown. (The total cooking time should be around 45–50 minutes.)

<u>To air-fry:</u> Preheat the air fryer to 350°F (180°C). Place the pork on an air-fryer pan lined with parchment paper and air-fry for 8 minutes, then remove the pan from the air fryer, flip the pork and baste with 2–3 tablespoons of the sauce. Air-fry for another 8 minutes.

Remove the pan from the air fryer. Reduce the temperature to 325°F (160°C). Flip the pork and baste with 2–3 tablespoons of the sauce. Air-fry for another 5–7 minutes.

Remove from the air fryer. Increase the temperature to 425°F (220°C). Flip the pork, baste with 2–3 tablespoons of the sauce and air-fry for a final 5–7 minutes until golden brown. (The total air-frying time should be 25–30 minutes.)

Remove the pork from the oven/air fryer. Leave to cool for 10 minutes, then slice against the grain into thick strips. Transfer to a large serving platter and pour over any remaining cooking juices. Serve with rice and sweetened soy sauce, if you like.

chapter

dumplings + wontons

four

Dumpling Deep Dive

A theory behind the origin of dumplings is that, once upon a time, villagers in a small town in China suffered frostbite on their ears from the long, harsh winter. Hoping to cure them, a doctor trained in Chinese medicine cooked up a mixture of traditional herbs with meat and sealed it in dough in the shape of an ear. The villagers loved these dumplings so much that they continued to eat them and they eventually turned into the meat- and vegetable-stuffed balls of deliciousness we enjoy today. The shape of dumplings also resembles money bags from ancient times, thus they are often served during Chinese New Year to usher in wealth and prosperity.

The general word used to refer to dumplings in Mandarin is *jiao zi* 饺子. This is the type of dumpling that you often find in the frozen aisle of grocery stores. However, there are dozens of dumpling varieties and ways to cook them. In China, we even use different words to describe them. For example, *shui jiao* 水饺 refers to dumplings boiled and cooked in water. *Guo tie* 锅贴 refers to dumplings that are pan-fried, also called pot stickers. Originated in Shanghai, we have *xiao long bao* 小笼包, soup dumplings steamed and wrapped with a thin dough. Even dim sum classics like *siu mai* 烧卖 (round open-faced dumplings) and *har gow* 虾饺 (shrimp dumplings wrapped in a translucent dough) are categorized as dumplings.

Depending on the region in China, people also use different fillings. In Northern China, people enjoy lamb- or beef-filled dumplings. In Western China, because of its proximity to the Middle East, people often add ground spices like cumin. Even the local preferences for the thickness of the dumpling wrapper varies. Hong Kongers enjoy dumplings with very thin wrappers, possibly because the warm tropical weather means people want lighter dumplings that don't weigh them down in the heat. In Northern China, the dumpling wrapper tends to be much thicker. Perhaps because the colder weather means people crave richer foods to help them stay warm.

Another type of dumpling that I cover in this book are wontons, *wun tun* 云吞. The wrapper is much thinner, sometimes has a yellowish hue from added egg yolks, and is made with slightly different ingredients than *jiao zi* pastry. Hong Kong-style wontons are filled with a mixture of shrimp and a small amount of pork for added fattiness and served in a soup. Shanghai also has its own style of wontons. Shanghainese wontons are much larger, filled with pork and vegetables, and typically do not add egg yolks to the wonton wrappers.

Many Chinese people no longer make dumplings from scratch because they are so readily available in supermarkets and restaurants. My grandmother never made her own dumplings! Having said that, nothing compares to serving up a platter of fresh homemade dumplings. It's the ultimate gesture of love. Not only do they taste better because you get to control the seasonings, it's also a fun activity to do with friends and family. The section below outlines a few basic guidelines to help you make the most delicious dumplings at home—way better than frozen supermarket ones.

Dumpling Dough

Time

30 minutes, plus 30 minutes resting

Ingredients

2 cups (250 g) dumpling flour (or all-purpose flour), plus extra for dusting (see Note 1)

1 tsp salt

about ½ cup (120 ml) hot water, plus 1–2 tsp extra, if needed

1 tsp neutral cooking oil

My trick for making delicious dumpling dough is to add hot water to the dough. The hot water slightly cooks off the proteins in the flour, which makes for a more tender dough. A drier dough (adding less water) will give you a slightly chewy dumpling skin. A wetter dough (adding more water) will give you a softer dumpling skin. It's up to you which you prefer.

Place the flour and salt in a bowl and mix to combine. Pour in the hot water and immediately mix with chopsticks or a fork, until a rough dough forms. If the dough is still quite dry, add 1–2 tablespoons of warm water until the dough sticks together (see Note 2).

Transfer the dough to a work surface, then add the oil. To knead, stretch and pull the dough apart then bring it back together again. Repeat for 5–7 minutes until a smooth dough forms. The dough should lightly spring back when you give it a poke. Wrap in plastic and set aside for at least 30 minutes—this makes it easier to roll out into thin wrappers. Alternatively, prepare a day ahead and leave the dough in the fridge overnight.

Lightly dust the work surface with flour. Divide the dough in half and set one half aside, wrapped in plastic wrap. Roll the dough into a long log, then cut with a knife or bench scraper into small pieces, each about 2 teaspoons in size. Roll each piece of dough into a ball shape, then press flat with the base of your palm. Dust the rolling pin with flour, then thinly roll each piece out into circles, 2 mm thick. Lightly dust flour between each dumpling wrapper to prevent them from sticking together. Repeat with the remaining dough.

To freeze, liberally dust each wrapper with cornstarch, then wrap with plastic wrap or place into a sealable plastic bag. They will keep in the freezer for up to 2–3 months. Defrost in the fridge overnight before use.

Notes

1: Classic dumplings (*jiao zi* 饺子) are made from plain wheat flour. I would highly recommend buying dumpling flour from an Asian supermarket because the flour is bleached and has a lower protein content. This means a softer, more tender and white-colored dumpling dough. Most dumpling flours in Asian supermarkets will either have an English label that says it's for dumplings, or a picture of a dumpling on it. However, if you're unable to find it, all-purpose flour will also work.

2: Depending on the brand of flour and the humidity in the air, the amount of water the dough needs will vary. I always start with a bit less water than the recipe states, then add more if necessary.

Wonton Dough

Makes about 30

Time
30 minutes, plus 30 minutes resting

Ingredients
9 oz (250 g) dumpling flour (or all-purpose flour), plus extra for dusting

1 tsp salt

1 egg yolk

1 tsp lye water (optional—see Note)

scant ½ cup–½ cup (105–115 ml) room-temperature water

Traditionally, chicken or duck eggs were added to wonton dough to give it a slightly yellow hue. Nowadays, most store-bought wonton wrappers have added food coloring to give them a bright yellow color. Wonton dough is a bit trickier to make than dumpling dough, but if you've made pasta from scratch before, this is a very similar process. Once wrapped, wontons look like bags of old Chinese money, which is why they symbolize wealth.

Place the flour and salt in a bowl and mix to combine. Add the egg yolk, lye water and water, and mix with chopsticks or a fork until a rough dough forms.

Transfer to a work surface and knead by stretching and pulling the dough apart, then bringing it back together. Repeat for 5–7 minutes until a smooth dough forms. The dough should lightly spring back when you give it a poke. If the dough feels very sticky, dust with flour. Wrap in plastic wrap and set aside for at least 30 minutes—this makes it easier to roll out into thin wrappers. Alternatively, prepare a day ahead and leave the dough in the fridge overnight.

Lightly dust the work surface with flour. Divide the dough in half and set one half aside, wrapped in the plastic wrap. Dust with flour, then thinly roll the dough into a large rectangle, around 2 mm thick. Dust with flour, then cut into squares, around 3½ x 3½ in (9 x 9 cm). Lightly dust flour between each wrapper to prevent them from sticking together. These are now ready for filling. Repeat with the other half of the dough.

To freeze, liberally dust each wrapper with cornstarch, then wrap with plastic wrap or place into a sealable plastic bag. They will keep in the freezer for up to 2–3 months. Defrost in the fridge overnight before use.

Note
Lye water is an alkaline solution that gives food a slightly chewy texture or a darker color. It's the same substance used in baked pretzels to give them their signature chewy texture and dark brown color. You can buy lye water in most Asian supermarkets, but if you can't find it you can omit it. Your wonton wrappers will just have a slightly softer, less chewy texture.

How to Fold Dumplings

There are many different ways to fold dumplings—this is just one of them.

Step 1
If using store-bought dumpling wrappers, wet the edges with cold water. If using homemade wrappers, skip this step.

Step 2
Add 1 heaped teaspoon of filling to the center of the wrapper.

Step 3
Fold the wrapper in half and press the top of the flaps together to seal, leaving the sides open.

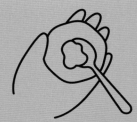
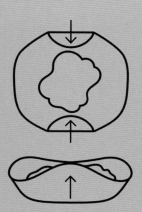

Step 4
Fold in the open sides to create a "T" shape on each side.

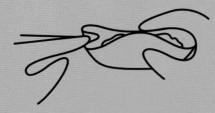

Step 5
Fold two of the short arms of each "T" (on the same side) in to meet each other and seal in the middle of the dumpling's edge. Bend the other arms of the "T" round slightly to make the dumpling curve gently.

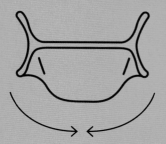
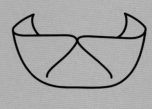

How to Fold Wontons

Step 1

If using store-bought wonton wrappers, wet the four edges with cold water. If using homemade wrappers, skip this step.

Step 2

Add 1 heaped teaspoon of filling to the center of the wrapper.

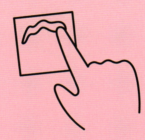

Step 3

Either...

Bring the four corners together, then lightly pinch the edges together on three sides just above the filling to seal. Fold the long sealed edge in to make the rectangle narrower, then bend the two short edges around your index finger to meet each other in the middle (leaving the folded long edge on the outside of the wonton) and slightly overlap the edges, pinching to seal. You will have a finger-sized hole in the middle of the wonton shape.

or

Fold the wrapper in half into a triangle and seal the two edges. Wet the two base corners of the triangle then bring them together around the filling, slightly overlapping the edges to seal.

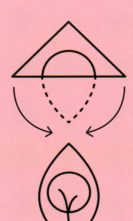

or

Simply bring the four corners of the wrapper together, then lightly pinch at the base to seal (right above the filling), which creates a "drawstring bag" shape.

How to Cook Dumplings

Boil

Lower the dumplings into a large pot of boiling water. Gently mix to prevent the dumplings from sticking to the bottom. For fresh dumplings, boil for 5–7 minutes until cooked through. For frozen dumplings, boil for 6–8 minutes.

Tip: Taste one before serving to make sure it's cooked through.

Steam

Prepare your steamer (see pages 20–1).

Place the dumplings in a lined steamer basket or on a plate, leaving space in between to prevent sticking. Steam over medium heat for 8–10 minutes, or until cooked through.

Pan Fry

Heat 1 teaspoon neutral cooking oil in a nonstick frying pan over medium heat. Add the dumplings to the pan, flat-side down (fresh or frozen). Fill the pan with a thin layer of water, less than halfway up the height of the dumpling. Cover with a lid and cook for 5–6 minutes until most of the liquid has evaporated. Remove the lid, then cook for a further 2–3 minutes, or until the bottom of the dumpling is crispy. You can add more oil at this point for a crispier dumpling.

How to Cook Wontons

Boil

Lower the wontons into a large pot of boiling water. Gently mix to prevent the wontons from sticking to the bottom. For fresh wontons, boil for 3–5 minutes until cooked through. For frozen wontons, boil for 4–6 minutes until cooked through.

Dumpling Sauces VE

Sour and Spicy

This is my personal go-to dipping sauce for wontons. Adding both vinegar and light soy gives it a delicious salty tang. This is also a wonderful sauce to go with a bowl of cold noodles.

Ingredients

1 tbsp black rice vinegar (or any vinegar)

1 tbsp light soy sauce

½ tsp sugar

2 tsp chile oil, or more to taste

1 scallion, thinly sliced

Method

In a small bowl, mix all the ingredients together. Serve as a dipping sauce for wontons or dumplings.

Fresh Chile and Soy

This incredibly simple soy and fresh chile dipping sauce was always on the dinner table. And I do mean always. We dip everything in this.

Ingredients

1 tbsp light soy sauce

½ tsp sugar

1 bird's-eye chile, finely chopped (or chile oil of choice)

Method

In a small bowl, mix all the ingredients together. Serve as a dipping sauce for anything.

Sesame Crunch

A creamy and crunchy dipping sauce to add even more oomph to your dumplings. If using peanut butter, I would opt for the crunchy stuff so you get a bite of peanut with every dumpling.

Ingredients

1 tbsp black rice vinegar (or any vinegar)

1 tbsp Chinese sesame paste (or peanut butter)

1 tbsp light soy sauce

½ tsp sugar

2 tsp chile oil, or more to taste

1 bunch of fresh cilantro, finely chopped

1 scallion, thinly sliced

1 tsp sesame seeds

pinch of crushed Sichuan peppercorns (optional)

Method

In a small bowl, mix all the ingredients together. Serve as a dipping sauce for wontons or dumplings.

白菜豬肉水饺

Pork and Cabbage Dumplings

Time

45 minutes

Ingredients

1½ cups (100 g) finely chopped cabbage

½ tsp salt, plus a pinch for the cabbage

9 oz (250 g) ground pork (at least 10% fat)

2 garlic cloves, finely chopped

1 small piece of fresh ginger root, peeled and finely chopped

2 scallions, finely chopped

2 tsp Shaoxing rice wine

2 tsp sesame oil

¼ tsp ground white pepper

1 egg white

1 tsp cornstarch (plus extra if freezing, see method)

2 tsp light soy sauce

½ tsp sugar

1 package of dumpling wrappers (or 30 homemade ones, see page 140)

Place the cabbage in a medium bowl, season with a pinch of salt and mix. Set aside for 10 minutes.

In a large bowl, mix together the pork, garlic, ginger, scallions, Shaoxing wine, sesame oil, white pepper, egg white, cornstarch, light soy sauce, sugar and ½ teaspoon salt.

Squeeze out the water that has come out of the cabbage. Add the cabbage to the pork bowl and mix.

Tip: At this stage, I recommend cooking a teaspoon of filling in a frying pan to check the seasoning. Adjust as needed.

Wet the edges of a dumpling wrapper with water. Place 1 heaped teaspoon of filling in the center of the wrapper, then fold to seal (see page 142). Repeat with the remaining wrappers and filling.

Cook according to the instructions on page 144.

To freeze, place the dumplings on a plate dusted with flour or cornstarch. Will keep frozen for up to 2–3 months. Cook straight from frozen (see page 144).

*Depending on size

Makes 30*

香菇豆腐水饺

Tofu, Mushroom and Spinach Dumplings VG

Time

45 minutes

Ingredients

7 oz (200 g) spinach

9 oz (250 g) firm tofu, pressed

6 shiitake mushrooms, rehydrated and finely chopped

2 garlic cloves, finely chopped

1 small piece of fresh ginger root, peeled and finely chopped

2 scallions, finely chopped

2 tsp Shaoxing rice wine

2 tsp sesame oil

½ tsp dark soy sauce

¼ tsp ground white pepper

1 egg

2 tsp cornstarch

2 tsp light soy sauce

2 tsp mushroom stir-fry sauce

½ tsp salt

½ tsp sugar

1 package of dumpling wrappers (or 30 homemade ones, see page 140)

Boil a kettle of water.

Place the spinach in a large colander. Over the kitchen sink, pour boiling water over the spinach until wilted. Rinse under cold running water. Squeeze and wring out most of the water from the spinach and transfer to a chopping board. Finely chop, then place in a large mixing bowl.

Crumble the tofu into the bowl, breaking apart any clumps into fine pieces. Add the shiitake mushrooms, garlic, ginger, scallions, Shaoxing wine, sesame oil, dark soy sauce, white pepper, egg, cornstarch, light soy sauce, mushroom stir-fry sauce, salt and sugar. Mix to combine.

Tip: At this stage, I recommend tasting a teaspoon of the filling to check the seasoning. Adjust as needed.

Wet the edges of a dumpling wrapper with water. Place 1 heaped teaspoon of filling in the center of the wrapper, then fold to seal (see page 142). Repeat with the remaining wrappers and filling.

Cook according to the instructions on page 144.

To freeze, place the dumplings on a plate dusted with flour or cornstarch. Will keep frozen for up to 2–3 months. Cook straight from frozen (see page 144).

*Depending on size

粟米雞肉水饺

Chicken and Corn Dumplings

Time

45 minutes

Ingredients

9 oz (250 g) ground chicken

⅓ cup (50 g) corn kernels

1 small piece of fresh ginger root, peeled and finely chopped

2 scallions, finely chopped

1 tsp light soy sauce

2 tsp sesame oil

1 tsp Shaoxing rice wine (optional)

¼ tsp ground white pepper

1 egg white

1 tsp cornstarch

½ tsp salt

1 tsp sugar

1 package of dumpling wrappers (or 30 homemade ones, see page 140)

*Depending on size

In a large bowl, mix together the chicken, corn, ginger, scallions, light soy sauce, sesame oil, Shaoxing wine, white pepper, egg white, cornstarch, salt and sugar.

Tip: At this stage, I recommend cooking a teaspoon of filling in a frying pan to check the seasoning. Adjust as needed.

Wet the edges of a dumpling wrapper with water. Place 1 heaped teaspoon of filling in the center of the wrapper, then fold to seal (see page 142). Repeat with the remaining wrappers and filling.

Cook according to the instructions on page 144.

To freeze, place the dumplings on a plate dusted with flour or cornstarch. Will keep frozen for up to 2–3 months. Cook straight from frozen (see page 144).

木耳豬肉云吞
Pork and Woodear Mushroom Wontons

Time

45 minutes

Ingredients

9 oz (250 g) ground pork (at least 20% fat)

1¾ oz (50 g) woodear mushrooms, rehydrated and thinly sliced

2 garlic cloves, finely chopped

1 small piece of fresh ginger root, peeled and finely chopped

2 tsp Shaoxing rice wine

2 tsp sesame oil

¼ tsp ground white pepper

1 egg white

1 tsp cornstarch

2 tsp light soy sauce

½ tsp salt

1 tsp sugar

1 package of large wonton wrappers (or homemade ones, see page 141, or store-bought wonton or dumpling wrappers)

*Depending on size

In a large bowl, mix together the pork, woodear mushrooms, garlic, ginger, Shaoxing wine, sesame oil, white pepper, egg white, cornstarch, light soy sauce, salt and sugar.

Tip: At this stage, I recommend cooking a teaspoon of filling in a frying pan to check the seasoning. Adjust as needed.

Wet the edges of a wonton wrapper with water. Place 1 heaped teaspoon of filling in the center of the wrapper, then fold to seal (see page 143). If using dumpling wrappers, follow instructions for dumpling folds (see page 142). Repeat with the remaining wrappers and filling.

To cook, gently lower the wontons into a large pot filled with boiling water. Cook for 3–4 minutes, or until cooked through. Drain, then transfer to a serving bowl. Serve with a dumpling sauce (see page 145) or simply some light soy sauce for dipping.

To freeze, place the wontons on a plate dusted with flour or cornstarch. Will keep frozen for up to 2–3 months. Cook straight from frozen (see page 144).

Makes 30*

鲜虾云吞
Shrimp Wontons PESC

Time

45 minutes

Ingredients

9 oz (250 g) raw shelled shrimp, deveined

2 scallions (white parts only), finely chopped

1 tsp sesame oil

½ tsp ground white pepper

1½ tsp cornstarch

2 tsp light soy sauce

½ tsp salt

½ tsp sugar

1 egg

1 package of large wonton wrappers (or homemade ones, see page 141, or store-bought wonton or dumpling wrappers)

*Depending on size

Place half of the shrimp in a food processor and blend into a rough paste. Add the remaining shrimp and pulse until very roughly chopped. (Alternatively, finely chop half of the shrimp by hand with a knife and very coarsely chop the remaining half.)

In a large bowl, mix together the shrimp mixture with the scallion whites, sesame oil, white pepper, cornstarch, light soy sauce, salt and sugar. Crack in the egg, then mix to combine. Transfer to the fridge to chill for 20 minutes—this will make the filling firmer and easier to shape the wontons.

Tip: At this stage, I recommend cooking a teaspoon of filling in a frying pan to check the seasoning. Adjust as needed.

Wet the edges of a wonton wrapper with water. Place 1 heaped teaspoon of filling in the center of the wrapper, then fold to seal (see page 143). If using dumpling wrappers, follow instructions for dumpling folds (see page 142). Repeat with the remaining wrappers and filling.

To cook, gently lower the wontons into a large pot filled with boiling water. Boil for 3–4 minutes, or until cooked through. Drain, then transfer to a serving bowl. Serve with a dumpling sauce or simply some light soy sauce for dipping.

To freeze, place the wontons on a plate dusted with flour or cornstarch. Will keep frozen for up to 2–3 months. Cook straight from frozen (see page 144).

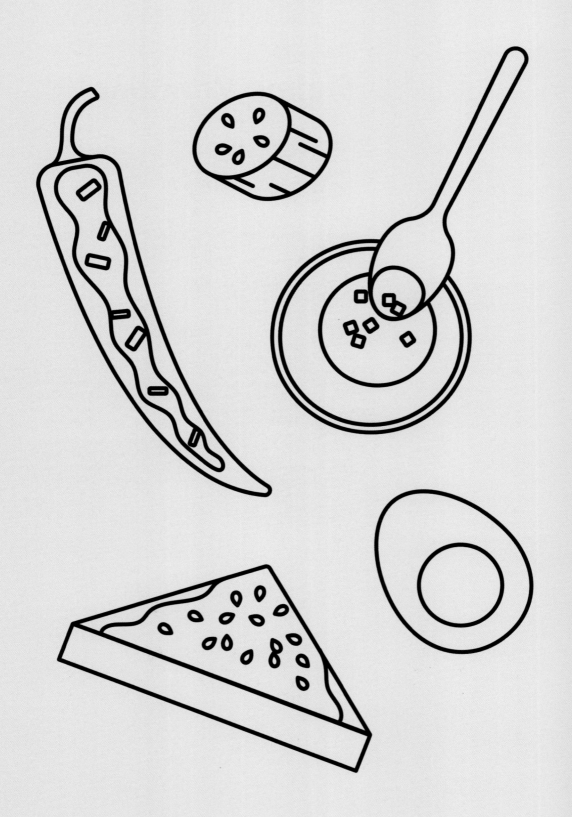

chapter

sides + snacks to share

five

Serves 2-4

干炒四季豆

Crispy Garlic Green Beans VE

Time
10–15 minutes

Ingredients
neutral cooking oil
7 oz (200 g) green beans, trimmed
5 garlic cloves, finely chopped
salt, to taste

This is a simplified and non-spicy version of crispy green beans that everyone in the family can enjoy. In order to achieve maximum garlic flavor, heat the oil and garlic from a cold pan. This will give the garlic more time to infuse into the oil without burning, thus more delicious garlicky goodness. *Pictured overleaf, far right.*

To shallow-fry the beans:
Cover the bottom of a frying pan or wok with a thin layer of oil and set over medium heat. Once hot, gently add the green beans and cook for 2–3 minutes until golden and crispy. Transfer the beans to a plate lined with paper towels to absorb any excess oil. Leave the oil in the pan to cool.

To air-fry the beans:
Preheat the air fryer to 400°F (200°C). Place the green beans on a lined air-fryer pan, then spray with oil and season with salt. Air-fry for 8–10 minutes until crispy.

To finish:
Either pour out excess oil from the cooled pan leaving just 2 tablespoons behind, or add 2 tablespoons of fresh oil to a cold wok or frying pan. Add the garlic to the pan and set over medium-low heat. Cook for 4–5 minutes until lightly golden and crispy (be careful not to burn the garlic). Add the fried green beans and toss to combine for 1–2 minutes. Season with salt.

Transfer to a plate and serve.

Serves 2-4

蒜蓉蚝油小白菜
Bok Choi with Soy Gravy VE

Time
10 minutes

Ingredients
1 lb (500 g) bok choi, halved lengthways

2 tsp neutral cooking oil

2 garlic cloves, finely chopped

1 small piece of fresh ginger root, peeled and finely chopped

For the sauce
scant ½ cup (100 ml) water or vegetable stock

1 tbsp Shaoxing rice wine

2 tsp mushroom stir-fry sauce

1 tsp light soy sauce

1 tsp dark soy sauce

1 tsp sesame oil

pinch of ground white pepper

1 tbsp cornstarch

This is a delicious vegetable dish that looks impressive, but is actually very easy to make. Crunchy Chinese greens are blanched, then covered with a silky, delicious soy glaze. I use bok choi here, but you can use whatever leafy greens you have on hand. I always take a few extra minutes to lay out the vegetables beautifully on a plate, just like they would in a Chinese restaurant. *Pictured overleaf, far left.*

Fill a wok or deep frying pan halfway with water and bring to a boil. Add the bok choi and simmer for 3–4 minutes until cooked through. Drain, then transfer to a serving platter.

In a small bowl, mix together the ingredients for the sauce.

Add the oil to the wok or pan and reheat over high heat. Add the garlic and ginger and cook for 1–2 minutes until fragrant. Add the sauce around the edges of the pan and bring to a boil. Cook for 2–3 minutes until thickened. Taste to adjust the seasoning.

Pour the sauce over the bok choi and serve immediately.

炒西兰花

Garlicky Stir-Fried Broccoli VE

Time
10 minutes

Ingredients

1 head of broccoli, cut into florets and the stalk thinly sliced into discs

2 tsp neutral cooking oil

3 garlic cloves, finely chopped

1 small piece of fresh ginger root, peeled and finely chopped

For the sauce

2 tsp cornstarch

scant ½ cup (100 ml) water

1 tsp light soy sauce

2 tsp mushroom stir-fry sauce

Growing up, this dish was a staple in my Cantonese home—delicious crunchy bites of broccoli covered in savory garlic sauce. Simple Chinese stir-fried vegetables are what I miss most when I'm away from home. I'm using broccoli in this recipe, but it works with other types of cruciferous vegetables, such as cauliflower, romesco cauliflower, cabbage or even Brussels sprouts. *Pictured on previous page, center.*

In a small bowl, mix together the ingredients for the sauce.

Bring a large wok or pot filled with water to a boil. Add the broccoli and cook for 3–4 minutes until just tender. Drain and set aside.

Add the oil to the wok or pot and reheat over high heat. Add the garlic and ginger and cook for 1–2 minutes until fragrant. Add the broccoli and toss to combine. Slowly pour in the sauce, while continuously stirring the broccoli. Cook for 1 minute until the sauce thickens and coats the broccoli.

Transfer to a large plate and serve immediately.

手撕包菜
Hand-Torn Cabbage Stir-Fry VE

Time
10–15 minutes

Ingredients

½ white cabbage

2 tsp neutral cooking oil

1 small piece of fresh ginger root, peeled and thinly sliced

3 garlic cloves, crushed

2 dried chiles, cut into large chunks (optional)

1 tbsp Shaoxing rice wine

2 tsp black rice vinegar

2 tsp light soy sauce

1 tsp sesame oil

½ tsp sugar

This is a popular Chinese stir-fry that you'll find throughout Shanghai and its neighboring provinces. Salty, slightly sour from the vinegar and mildly spicy from the dried chiles, it's an easy dish that also stands up on its own and can accompany any meal.

Tear the cabbage with your hands into large pieces, around 2 in (5 cm) in size.

Heat the oil in a large wok or frying pan over high heat. Add the ginger and garlic and cook for 1–2 minutes until fragrant. Add the cabbage and dried chiles, and cook for 3–4 minutes, stirring frequently.

Add the rice wine around the edges of the pan and cook for 4–6 minutes until the cabbage has softened but still retains a bite. If it starts to burn, add a small splash of water. Add the remaining seasonings and mix to combine. Taste to adjust the seasoning.

Transfer to a large plate and serve.

拍黄瓜
Smacked Cucumber Salad VE

There are two tricks to getting a delicious cucumber salad. First, you need to smack the cucumber to get those rough edges for the sauce to cling to. Second, salt the cucumbers for a few minutes beforehand to draw out excess cucumber juices. This will help the cucumber absorb more of the dressing.

Time
10 minutes

Ingredients
2 small Persian or mini cucumbers
½ tsp salt
1 scallion, thinly sliced
1 garlic clove, finely chopped
½ tsp sugar
2 tsp black rice vinegar
1 tsp light soy sauce
1 tsp sesame oil

To garnish
2 tsp sesame seeds
small handful of fresh cilantro
drizzle of chile oil

Trim the ends off the cucumbers. Tilt the knife parallel to the chopping board, then bash the cucumbers until the flesh starts to split open. Roughly chop, at an angle, into ¾ in (2 cm) wide chunks. Place in a medium bowl and toss with the salt. Set aside for 5 minutes, or until the salt has drawn out some water from the cucumbers.

Drain the water from the cucumbers. Add the sliced scallion, garlic, sugar, black rice vinegar, light soy sauce and sesame oil. Mix to combine. Taste to adjust the seasonings.

Place on a plate and garnish with the sesame seeds, cilantro and a drizzle of chile oil.

煎釀辣椒

Stuffed Chile Peppers

PESC

Time
20 minutes

Ingredients

6½ oz (180 g) raw shelled shrimp, deveined (or ground pork, or a combination)

½ tsp sugar

½ tsp salt

1½ tsp light soy sauce

½ tsp ground white pepper

2 tsp cornstarch, plus extra for dusting

2 tbsp water

2 scallions, thinly sliced

5–6 long chile peppers, deseeded and halved lengthways (see Note)

1 tbsp neutral cooking oil

For the dipping sauce (optional)

2 tbsp light soy sauce

1 red chile (deseeded for less heat, if you wish), very thinly sliced

---

I always ask my grandma to make these stuffed peppers when I go over for dinner. It's a homestyle version of a popular street snack sold in Hong Kong—vegetables like eggplants, peppers, or long chiles, stuffed with a savory meat filling. My grandma uses a mix of pork and shrimp, but feel free to use one or the other. With the type of chile peppers my grandma uses, it's always a game of Russian roulette, because most of the peppers are mild, but sometimes you get a super spicy one (and those are my favorite).

In a blender or food processor, combine the shrimp (and/or pork), sugar, salt, light soy sauce, white pepper, cornstarch and water. Blend until a smooth, jelly-like paste forms, 3–5 minutes (see Note).

Transfer the filling to a medium bowl and stir in the scallions. Perhaps fry off a small piece of the filling to check the seasonings (see Note). Chill the filling in the fridge while you prepare the peppers and dipping sauce.

Lightly dust the inside of the peppers with cornstarch—this will help the filling stick to the peppers. Stuff the peppers evenly with the filling, making sure the top is flat and even.

Heat the oil in a nonstick frying pan over medium heat. In batches, add the peppers to the pan, filling-side down. Cook for 4–6 minutes until golden brown and the filling is cooked through, then flip and cook on the other sides for 1–2 minutes (you want the peppers to retain some bite).

Transfer the peppers to a large serving platter and serve either with the dipping sauce or on their own.

Notes

If using bell peppers, use 2–3 medium bell peppers cut into large wedges, about 2 in (5 cm) wide.

My grandma emphasises blending or mixing the filling until it turns from a paste into a bouncy jelly. This will give your stuffed peppers a slightly springy texture.

My tip for making any filling is to cook a teaspoon or so in a frying pan first, then taste and adjust the seasoning.

Makes 10–20*

春卷
Vegetable Spring Rolls VE

Time
20–30 minutes

Ingredients

neutral cooking oil, for frying or brushing

2 carrots, thinly sliced

1 small cabbage (any variety), thinly shredded

10½ oz (300 g) beansprouts, rinsed

3 garlic cloves, finely chopped

1 small piece of fresh ginger root, peeled and finely chopped

2 tsp light soy sauce

2 tsp sesame oil

½ tsp sugar

salt and ground white pepper, to taste

2 tsp cornstarch

2 tbsp water

1 package of frozen spring roll pastry (10 in/25 cm squares for large rolls, or smaller size will work too), defrosted

4 tbsp Thai sweet chile sauce, for dipping

*Makes around 10 large or 20 small rolls

A crowd favorite that's also super easy to make. I love my spring rolls packed with as many vegetables as possible. You can use whatever vegetables you want, just make sure they're all thinly sliced so you get a bit of every vegetable with each bite. I keep it classic and serve these with Thai sweet chile sauce on the side.

Heat 2 teaspoons of oil in a large wok or frying pan over medium-low heat. Add the carrot and cabbage, and cook for about 5 minutes until softened (you want to cook the vegetables without getting too much browning). Add the beansprouts and cook for about 2 minutes until wilted. Add the garlic and ginger and cook for a minute, then add the light soy sauce, sesame oil, sugar, salt and white pepper. Taste to adjust the seasoning. Transfer to a large bowl and set aside to cool slightly.

In a small bowl, mix together the cornstarch and water. This acts as a glue to help the pastry stick together.

Place a sheet of spring roll pastry on a work surface, with the corner pointing downwards (*pictured on page 168*). Place another sheet on top, slightly upwards and adjacent (so the sheets are not directly on top of one other). Place 3–4 tablespoons of filling on the lower third of the pastry. Using your fingers, wet the edges of the pastry with the glue. Tightly roll the pastry halfway up, then bring the left and right corners to the center and continue rolling into a log shape. If the pastry doesn't stick, wet the edges with more glue. Continue with the remaining pastry sheets and filling.

(You can freeze the spring rolls on a large plate or tray lined with parchment paper and they will keep for up to 1 month. Cook from frozen.)

To air-fry:

Preheat the air fryer to 400°F (200°C). Place the spring rolls on a lined air-fryer pan and brush or spray with cooking oil. Air-fry for 12–15 minutes until crispy on the outside (the pastry will get crispy, but the color will not be as dark brown as deep-fried spring rolls).

To deep-fry:

Fill a deep frying pan or wok halfway with cooking oil and set over medium heat. When the oil is hot enough (see Note), gently lower the spring rolls into the hot oil, in batches. Cook for 5–7 minutes, turning occasionally, until golden brown all over. Repeat with the remaining spring rolls. Drain on a wire rack or a plate lined with paper towels.

Place the spring rolls on a chopping board and cut in half at an angle (optional). Serve on a large platter with Thai sweet chile sauce on the side for dipping.

Note

To test if the oil is hot enough, insert a wooden chopstick/utensil into the oil. If it immediately sizzles, then the oil is hot enough. While deep-frying, if the oil gets too hot, reduce the heat or add a small splash of cold oil to bring the temperature of the oil down quickly.

上汤娃娃菜
Braised Chinese Cabbage with Smoked Bacon

This dish is sure to warm you up on a cold winter night. This Shanghainese dish is traditionally made with a dry-cured ham called *jin hua huo tui* 金華火腿. It has a distinct salty and slightly smoky flavor that goes very well with leafy vegetables. This ham is quite difficult to find internationally, however an excellent substitute is smoked bacon. I've added a cornstarch slurry to create a glaze, but feel free to skip it for a more brothy dish.

Time
20 minutes

Ingredients
1 tsp neutral cooking oil

1¾ oz (50 g) smoked bacon, thinly sliced

2 garlic cloves, crushed

1 large piece of fresh ginger root, peeled and sliced into thin discs

1 tbsp Shaoxing rice wine

1 small Chinese cabbage (Napa cabbage), core removed and leaves separated

1¼ cups (300 ml) low-sodium chicken stock

For the cornstarch slurry
1 tbsp cornstarch

3½ tbsp water

Heat the oil in a large wok or pot (that has a lid) over medium heat. Add the bacon and cook for 3–4 minutes until some of the fat has rendered out. Add the garlic and ginger, and cook for 1 minute. Add the rice wine, cabbage and chicken stock, and mix to combine. Cover and simmer for 10–12 minutes until the cabbage is tender.

In a small bowl, mix together the cornstarch and water.

Turn the heat to low, then slowly pour in the cornstarch slurry, while continuously stirring. Bring to a boil and cook for 1–2 minutes until the sauce thickens. Taste to adjust the seasoning.

Transfer to a large bowl and serve.

蒜蓉炒生菜

Ginger and Garlic Stir-Fried Lettuce VE

Time

5 minutes

Ingredients

2 tsp neutral cooking oil

3 garlic cloves, finely chopped

1 small piece of fresh ginger root, peeled and finely chopped

7 oz (200 g) gem lettuce or romaine (or any leafy green), trimmed and cut in half

½ tsp salt

¼ tsp sugar

When you order a plate of stir-fried greens in a Chinese restaurant, they usually give you two options: either blanched and served with oyster sauce, or stir-fried with ginger and garlic. This is my recipe for the ginger and garlic version. My tip is to make sure you season the dish only at the very end, otherwise the salt and sugar will draw out too much moisture and cause the dish to turn watery.

Heat the oil in a wok or frying pan over high heat. Add the garlic and ginger, and cook for 1–2 minutes until fragrant. Add the lettuce and cook for 2–3 minutes, tossing to combine, until slightly wilted. Season with the salt and sugar.

Transfer to a large plate and serve.

Note

You can use this method for other leafy greens, such as kale, bok choi and watercress. However, you might have to add a few extra minutes of stir-frying to make sure the vegetables are cooked through.

半生熟茶叶蛋
Soft-Boiled Tea Eggs VG

Time
15 minutes, plus
6 hours–2 days marinating

Ingredients
4 eggs

For the tea marinade
1⅔ cups (400 ml) water
2 tbsp light soy sauce
1 tbsp dark soy sauce
2 bay leaves
1 cinnamon stick
2 tbsp sugar
1 black tea bag (Earl Grey, English Breakfast, Assam, etc.)

Tea eggs are a snack sold in all street stalls and convenience stores in China. They're hard-boiled eggs simmered in a savory tea marinade with a slightly cracked shell, giving the egg whites a beautiful marbled appearance. In my recipe, I leave the eggs to soak up the marinade overnight, instead of cooking in the sauce. I also peel my eggs for ease and soft-boil them, simply because I love a gooey yolk. However, you can do it the traditional way and place slightly cracked hard-boiled eggs into the marinade.

Bring a pot of water to a boil. Gently lower in the eggs and boil for 6 minutes for soft-boiled, or 7 minutes for hard-boiled. Use a slotted spoon to transfer the eggs to a bowl of ice-cold water and set aside. Once cooled, peel the eggs or gently crack the egg shell.

In a small saucepan, combine all of the ingredients for the marinade. Bring to a boil, then simmer for 2–3 minutes until the sugar has dissolved. Transfer to an airtight container and set aside to cool.

Once the marinade has slightly cooled, add the eggs to it. Transfer to the fridge and leave to marinate for at least 6 hours, or up to 2 days.

Enjoy the eggs on their own, or with toast or a fresh bowl of rice.

Note
It is much easier to peel slighter older boiled eggs than super-fresh eggs. I usually make this dish a few days after I've bought a new carton of eggs. That way, I don't give myself a headache trying to peel fresh eggs.

冻豆腐
Chilled Soy Tofu VE

Time
5 minutes

Ingredients

1 x 12 oz (350 g) block of silken tofu, chilled and drained

1 very small piece of fresh ginger root, peeled and finely grated

1 scallion, thinly sliced

1 tbsp light soy sauce

1 tsp sesame oil

My dad made this dish all the time when I was growing up. It's an easy and refreshing dish to serve at the table, with little to no effort. You can use medium-firm tofu if you like, but I prefer silken tofu for this recipe. The tofu is the star of the dish, so try to find high-quality tofu from an Asian supermarket for the best results.

Gently place the silken tofu on a serving plate. Top with the grated ginger and sprinkle over the scallions. Drizzle over the light soy sauce and sesame oil. Serve cold.

Note
My dad usually serves the block of tofu whole, with a serving spoon on the side to scoop up some of the tofu with the sauce. However, you can also slice the tofu into large wedges before serving.

虾多士
Shrimp Toast PESC

Time
20 minutes

Ingredients

6 oz (165 g) raw shelled shrimp, deveined

2 scallions, thinly sliced

1 egg white

1 tsp sesame oil

2 tsp cornstarch

½ tsp sugar

salt and ground white pepper

4 tbsp sesame seeds

4 slices of white bread

neutral cooking oil

4 tbsp Thai sweet chile sauce, for dipping

The story goes that this snack was originally created for foreigners in Hong Kong. However, locals tried it and loved it as well. Now you'll find shrimp toast served in many dim sum restaurants as an appetizer. My uncle makes it in an air fryer with store-bought shrimp paste (a popular local product used to make shrimp balls for hotpot). He even coats the bread with garlic butter before spreading on the shrimp paste to turn it into a garlic-bread-shrimp-toast mash-up.

In a food processor or blender, blend half of the shrimp until finely chopped. Transfer to a large bowl. Roughly chop the remaining shrimp and add it to the bowl. Add the scallions, egg white, sesame oil, cornstarch and sugar. Season with salt and white pepper to taste and mix to combine (see Note).

Place the sesame seeds onto a shallow plate. Line an air-fryer pan or tray with parchment paper.

Spread the shrimp mixture evenly over the bread slices, then dip them, shrimp-side down, into the sesame seeds to evenly coat. Transfer to the lined pan or tray.

To air-fry:

Preheat the air fryer to 400°F (200°C). Spray the shrimp toasts with oil. Air-fry for 8–10 minutes, or until the shrimp mixture is cooked through and the sesame seeds are golden.

To deep-fry:

Fill a wok or deep frying pan halfway with cooking oil and set over medium heat. When the oil is hot enough (see Note), gently lower the shrimp toasts into the oil, in batches. Cook for 2–3 minutes until golden brown, then flip and cook for another 2–3 minutes until golden brown and cooked through. Using tongs or a slotted spoon, transfer to a wire rack or a plate lined with paper towels.

Slice the toasts into smaller triangles and place on a large serving platter. Serve with Thai sweet chile sauce on the side for dipping.

Notes

Whenever I make a filling of any kind, I always cook off a teaspoon in a frying pan, then taste to check the seasoning before continuing to cook my dish.

To test if the oil is hot enough, insert a wooden chopstick/utensil into the oil. If it immediately sizzles, then the oil is hot enough. While deep-frying, if the oil gets too hot, reduce the heat or add a small splash of cold oil to bring the temperature of the oil down.

Makes 6

葱油饼
Scallion Pancakes VE

Time

1 hour 10 minutes, plus 2 hours or overnight resting

Ingredients

For the dough

5 cups (600 g) all-purpose flour, plus extra for dusting

1 tsp salt

1 cup (250 ml) hot water

⅔ cup (160 ml) room-temperature water

For the filling

8–10 scallions, thinly sliced (white and green parts separated)

8 tbsp neutral cooking oil

5 tbsp all-purpose flour, or as needed

¾ tsp salt

One of Shanghai's most popular snacks are *cong you bing*, flaky layered flatbreads stuffed with scallions, then pan-fried until crispy on the outside and slightly chewy in the middle. I have so many memories of hopping off my bike to buy a stack of these after smelling them from all the way down the street. Over the years, I've perfected this recipe to create an incredibly flaky pancake packed with scallion flavor.

To make the dough, place the flour and salt in a mixing bowl and stir to combine. Pour in the hot water and mix until the water is evenly distributed (the dough should still be very dry at this point). Add the room-temperature water and mix until a rough dough forms. Tip the dough out onto a work surface and knead for 3–5 minutes until smooth. Cover with plastic wrap and leave to rest for 2 hours, or overnight for best results.

For the filling, place the scallion whites in a small saucepan along with the oil. Simmer over low heat for 8–10 minutes to slowly infuse the oil.

Meanwhile, place the scallion greens in a bowl, add the flour and salt, and mix. Pour the hot scallion oil over the flour and mix until a thick paste forms.

Divide the dough into 6 pieces and loosely cover with plastic wrap. With a rolling pin, roll a piece of dough into a thin rectangular sheet, about ¼ in (5 mm) thick.

Spread about 2 large spoonfuls of filling evenly over the dough, leaving a small lip around the edges. Starting from the longest side of the rectangle, tightly roll the dough into a log. Swirl the dough into a tight coil shape, starting at each end and coiling in the opposite direction (this creates a coiled "S" shape; *pictured on page 182*). Flip the coils on top of each other, then cover with plastic wrap and set aside. Repeat with the remaining pieces of dough and filling.

Return to the first coil and roll it out to a thin disc, around ½ in (1.5 cm) thick. Repeat with the remaining dough coils. (You can freeze them at this stage by wrapping the uncooked dough in parchment paper. Cook straight from frozen.)

Heat a medium frying pan (that has a lid) over medium heat. Add the pancake and cook for 2–3 minutes until golden brown. Cover the pan with a lid and cook for a further 3–4 minutes. Flip the pancake and cook for another 3–4 minutes until golden brown, crispy and cooked through. If you like, you can use two spatulas to scrunch up the sides of the pancake and make it flakier. Repeat with the remaining pancakes.

Serve on its own or with light soy sauce for dipping.

sides + snacks to share

chapter

sauces + condiments

seven

Serves 4

辣椒酱
Easy Chile Sauce VG

Time
10 minutes, plus
1–4 days fermentation

Ingredients
1 lb (500 g) mixed red peppers, deseeded and roughly chopped (see Note)

1½ tsp salt

2½ tsp sugar

4 tsp distilled white vinegar (or any kind)

This is a simple alternative chile sauce for those of you who like chile sauce, but don't necessarily enjoy how spicy or oily some can be. This recipe comes together in less than 10 minutes but also has the added tangy flavor of fermentation. It uses mainly bell peppers, so you can control the amount of spice you want. It has a fresh, tangy flavor and is wonderful to drizzle over noodles, rice or eggs, or even mixed with mayonnaise for a chile mayo.

Add all the ingredients to a food processor or blender and blend until roughly chopped (or smooth if you prefer a smoother chile sauce).

Place into an airtight container or jar and set aside in a cool dry place for 1–2 days to ferment. If you want a more sour chile sauce, ferment for another 1–2 days.

Transfer to the fridge and enjoy with whatever you like. This sauce will keep for up to 2 months.

Note
I like to use a mix of different types of peppers to add more depth to the chile sauce. I often add small Thai red chiles for heat, but you can use whatever variety is available to you. If you live in a colder climate, the fermentation might take longer, so taste it every day to check the flavor until it is to your liking.

Serves 4

薑葱蓉

Ginger and Scallion Sauce VE OPTION

Time
8–10 minutes

Ingredients

⅓ cup (80 ml) neutral cooking oil

1 large piece of fresh ginger root, peeled and finely grated

6 scallions, thinly sliced

½ tsp sugar

½ tsp salt

1–2 tbsp chicken fat (optional)

This sauce, served alongside my grandmother's White-Cut Chicken (see page 102), is something that we enjoy at almost every family gathering. Her secret is stirring in a bit of chicken fat for extra flavor. Unlike my grandmother, I don't have a jar of chicken fat in the fridge. Instead, I skim off some of the fat that has risen to the top of the chicken steaming juices during cooking. But this is optional—you can serve the sauce without added fat, alongside noodles or rice. *Pictured overleaf, far left.*

Heat the oil in a frying pan over medium-high heat. Add the ginger and cook for 3–4 minutes until fragrant. Add the scallions and cook for 3–4 minutes until softened. Transfer to a medium bowl and add the sugar and salt. Mix to combine. Taste to adjust the seasoning.

If serving alongside White-Cut Chicken, add 1–2 tablespoons of chicken fat, skimmed from the steaming juices.

If serving on its own, enjoy with a bowl of freshly cooked noodles or rice. It's also great with Pork Chop Rice (see page 28).

葱頭油
Shallot Crisp VE

Time
15–20 minutes

Ingredients
8 shallots, thinly sliced into half-moons

1¼ cups (300 ml) neutral cooking oil

2 tbsp light soy sauce

4 tsp dark soy sauce

2 tsp sesame oil

1 tsp salt

1 tsp sugar

In a Chinese supermarket, right next to the chile oils, you'll find a wide array of flavored oils. One of my favorites is shallot oil, an infused oil with bits of fried shallot that you can use as a flavor booster for whatever you're cooking. I add a spoonful of shallot oil as a finishing touch to dishes like fried rice, noodles or vegetables, or even over my fried eggs in the morning. *Pictured bottom center.*

Place the shallots and oil in a small saucepan, set over low heat, and cook for 15–20 minutes until golden brown. Reduce the heat if the shallots brown too quickly.

Remove from the heat and add the remaining ingredients. Taste to adjust the seasonings. Leave to cool, then transfer to an airtight container or jar. It will keep for up to 2 weeks.

Great with rice or noodles, or drizzled over cooked meats or scrambled eggs.

Makes 1½ cups (350 ml)

辣椒油
Basic Chile Oil VE

Time
15 minutes

Ingredients

For the infused oil
1¼ cups (300 ml) neutral cooking oil

3 garlic cloves, crushed

2 shallots, thinly sliced

1 large piece of fresh ginger root, peeled and thinly sliced into discs

3 scallions, cut into thirds

2 star anise

1 cinnamon stick

4 bay leaves

1 tbsp Sichuan peppercorns

1 tbsp black peppercorns

To finish
3 tbsp chile powder

3 tbsp crushed red pepper flakes

2 tbsp sesame seeds

1–2 tsp salt

1–2 tsp sugar

2 tbsp water

2–3 tbsp black rice vinegar (or substitute any vinegar you have, although the flavor will be different)

1 tbsp sesame oil (optional)

There are so many types of chile oil in China: spicy and numbing, or sweet and salty, smooth or crunchy. Hong Kongers are not known for their spice tolerance, even though I personally love a bit of kick in my chile oil. My recipe is an easy, all-purpose chile oil that you can use with everything. The amount of chile powder/flakes you add is up to you—if you want a milder heat, just add less. If you're missing some of the spices, don't worry about it. Just use what you have in your pantry. *Pictured on page 189, top center.*

Heat the neutral oil in a medium saucepan over medium heat (to about 240°F/115°C). Add the garlic, shallots, ginger, scallions, star anise, cinnamon, bay leaves, Sichuan and black peppercorns. Cook for 8–10 minutes until light golden brown.

Place the chile powder, crushed red pepper flakes, sesame seeds, salt and sugar in a heatproof bowl. Add the water and mix until well combined (the water prevents the chile from burning and turning bitter in the hot oil).

Pour the hot infused oil through a sieve into the chile mixture. The chile should sizzle immediately. Add the vinegar and sesame oil, and leave to sizzle. Once slightly cooled, mix to combine. Taste to adjust the seasoning.

This is great with noodles, fried rice or in a dipping sauce with dumplings.

Note
There are endless variations to this chile oil recipe. If you want, you can skip the vinegar and keep it basic. Experimenting with different brands of chile flakes and chile powder will also give you a slightly different flavor. Here is a list of other ingredients that you can add to your chile oil:

Variations/Additions:
2–4 tbsp fried garlic, shallots or onions (sold in many supermarkets)

2–4 tbsp chopped peanuts

½–1 tsp ground white pepper

1–2 tsp garlic/onion powder

1–2 tsp Chinese five spice

1–2 tsp ground Sichuan peppercorns

sauces + condiments

Makes 1⅓ cups (320 ml)

甜豉油
Sweet Soy Sauce VE

Time
10 minutes

Ingredients

4 tsp neutral cooking oil

3 in (8 cm) piece of fresh ginger root, peeled and thinly sliced into discs

2 shallots, quartered (or 1 red onion)

4 garlic cloves, crushed

2 tbsp Shaoxing rice wine

¼ cup (60 ml) light soy sauce

¼ cup (60 ml) dark soy sauce

2 tbsp sugar

½ cup (120 ml) water

The soy sauce aisle in Chinese supermarkets is filled with dozens of soy sauce options, made from different types of soybeans, with varying fermentation periods and levels of sweetness. There are even soy sauces specifically made for cooking seafood, poultry and for dipping dim sum. My recipe infuses regular store-bought soy sauce with even more flavor. It's an all-purpose seasoning you can enjoy with anything, from noodles to plain rice to drizzling over dumplings or fried eggs. *Pictured on page 189, top right.*

Heat the oil in a medium saucepan over high heat. Add the ginger, shallot and garlic, and cook for 3–4 minutes until fragrant and lightly charred. Add the rest of the ingredients to the pan and cook for 2–3 minutes until boiling, then remove from the heat. Leave to cool slightly, then transfer to jars or an airtight container. It will keep in the fridge for up to 1 week.

Note
I don't strain my soy sauce because I like the ingredients to continue infusing into the sauce. However, you can strain the sauce to prolong its shelf life and keep in an airtight container in the fridge for up to 2 weeks.

chapter

desserts

eight

Serves 4

芒果糯米饭
Mango Sticky Rice VE

Time
30–35 minutes, plus
3–4 hours or overnight soaking

Ingredients
1 cup (200 g) glutinous rice, soaked (see Note)

1 x 14 oz (400 ml) can of full-fat coconut milk

2½ tbsp sugar, or more to taste

½ tsp salt

1 large mango

For the cornstarch slurry
1 tsp cornstarch

1 tbsp water

Cantonese people love their mango desserts. This is traditionally a Thai dessert, but it has become so popular and well-loved that it's sold in almost all Hong Kong dessert shops. I learned how to make coconut sticky rice from an old Thai colleague, who used to own a chain of dessert shops in Thailand.

Place the rice in a large bowl and cover with cold water. Leave to soak for 3–4 hours minimum, or ideally overnight.

Prepare a steamer (see pages 20–1).

Drain the soaked rice, place it on a tea towel or cheesecloth and loosely wrap it into a parcel. Place in the steamer and steam on medium heat for 15–20 minutes until cooked through. If the water runs out halfway, add more boiling water to the steamer.

Add the coconut milk, sugar and salt to a small saucepan and set over medium heat. Simmer for 2–3 minutes until the sugar has dissolved. Remove from the heat.

Transfer the cooked glutinous rice to a large mixing bowl. Pour over ⅔ cup (160 ml) of the warm coconut milk mixture. Leave the rice to absorb the liquid for at least 10–15 minutes.

Meanwhile, in a small bowl, mix together the ingredients for the cornstarch slurry. Reheat the remaining coconut milk mixture in the saucepan over medium heat. Remove from the heat, then slowly pour in the cornstarch slurry, while continuously stirring. Place back on the heat and cook for 1–2 minutes until thickened. Taste to adjust for sweetness, adding more sugar for a sweeter glaze.

Halve the mango lengthways, running the knife along the seed. Scoop out the mango flesh from each half with a metal spoon, then thinly slice into ¾ in (2 cm) wedges. Arrange on the side of 4 plates.

Serve the glutinous rice on plates alongside the mango slices. Pour over the coconut glaze.

Note
This recipe uses glutinous rice, often called sticky rice or Thai sticky rice. This variety of rice is very different to Japanese sushi rice, which is confusingly also called sticky rice. Glutinous rice is a common ingredient in Cantonese desserts and dim sum dishes, but also widely eaten throughout Asia in savory dishes and desserts. Soaking the rice beforehand ensures even cooking, and cuts the cooking time by half.

杨枝甘露
Mango Pomelo Sago Pudding

Time
15–20 minutes

Ingredients

⅔ cup (100 g) sago pearls

10½ oz (300 g) mango flesh (from around 2–3 mangoes), cut into large cubes (see Note)

⅓ cup (80 g) evaporated milk

scant ½ cup (100 ml) fresh milk (any kind)

scant ½ cup (100 ml) full-fat coconut milk

2–4 tbsp condensed milk (add more if you like it sweeter)

7 oz (200 g) pink or white pomelo flesh (or grapefruit), torn into small pieces

This is a quintessential Cantonese dessert found in all Hong Kong dessert shops. The Chinese name of the dish is much more poetic than its English translation. The name means "magical dew from the willow tree," and comes from a story about one of the most cherished goddesses in China, Guanyin (the goddess of compassion). This mango dessert, which is more like a cold soup than a pudding, is so refreshing it is indeed like the magic of Guanyin.

Bring a pot of water to a boil. Add the sago pearls and cook for 10–12 minutes until only a small white dot remains in the center of the pearls. Drain and rinse under running cold water, then transfer to a bowl of ice-cold water and set aside.

Place one-third (3½ oz/100 g) of the mango flesh into a blender or food processor and blend until smooth. Transfer to a large mixing bowl. Add the evaporated milk, fresh milk, coconut milk and condensed milk, and whisk to combine.

When ready to serve, add the sago and pomelo to the milk mixture and stir to combine. Divide the mixture among 4–6 bowls and garnish with the remaining mango cubes.

Notes

Mango is one of the main ingredients in this dessert, so it's important to use ripe sweet mangoes. In Hong Kong, people often use mangoes from Thailand or the Philippines, but you can use whatever mangoes are available to you. Just make sure to wait for them to ripen, if not overripen, before use.

The sago and mango coconut mixtures can be prepared ahead of time and kept separately in the fridge for 2–3 days. Place the cooked sago pearls in a container filled with cold water to prevent them from sticking to each other.

汤圆
Tang Yuan in Sweet Ginger Soup VE

Tang yuan are chewy glutinous rice balls, similar to mochi, stuffed with sweet fillings like red bean paste, peanuts or sesame. They're often served during Lunar New Year because the round shape represents family and togetherness. My parents always have a pack in the freezer ready to go whenever a craving hits. This is a simplified version that uses store-bought nut butter for ease.

Time

35 minutes, plus
30 minutes chilling

Ingredients

For the filling

3 tbsp crunchy peanut butter

¼ cup (40 g) peanuts, finely chopped

2 tbsp water (at room temperature)

2 tbsp salted butter, melted

2–3 tsp sugar (any type) (omit if using sweetened peanut butter)

For the dough

1⅔ cups (200 g) glutinous rice flour, or as needed (see note)

scant ½ cup (100–110 ml) water, at room temperature (see Note)

For the ginger soup

2½ cups (600 ml) water

1 small piece of fresh ginger root, peeled and sliced into thin discs

2–3 tbsp brown sugar

In a small bowl, mix together the ingredients for the filling. Taste to adjust for sweetness. Transfer the filling to a large piece of plastic wrap and roll into a log, around ½ in (1.5 cm) in diameter. Place in the freezer and chill for at least 30 minutes. (You can do this step ahead of time and freeze the filling for up to 1 month.)

To make the dough, place the glutinous rice flour in a large bowl. Add the water (see Note) and mix until a dough forms. The dough should feel tacky but should not stick to your hands.

Roll just 2 teaspoons of the dough into a ball, then gently pat into a flat disc. Bring a small saucepan of water to a boil. Lower the disc of dough into the water and cook for 1–2 minutes until it floats to the surface. Remove with a slotted spoon and add back into the remaining dough. Knead until evenly combined. This step gives you a smoother, chewier dough.

The dough should stretch without breaking. If it feels too sticky, add another 1 tablespoon of glutinous rice flour. Set aside.

Remove the filling from the freezer, cut the log into ½ in (1 cm) pieces and roll into balls. Return the balls to the freezer while you roll out the dough.

Roll 1 heaped teaspoon-sized piece of dough into a ball. Gently make a hole in the middle and stuff with a ball of filling. Roll back into a ball. Repeat with the remaining dough and filling. (You can freeze your tang yuan at this point and cook them another time.)

Combine all the ginger soup ingredients in a pot. Bring to a boil, then reduce to a simmer. Taste to adjust for sweetness. Lower the tang yuan into the soup, stirring to prevent sticking. Cook for 3–4 minutes or until the tang yuan float to the surface.

Divide among small bowls and serve immediately.

Note

This recipe calls for glutinous rice flour, sometimes called sweet rice flour. Made from glutinous rice, the flour has a signature chewy and sticky texture. Plain rice flour is made from long-grain rice, so it doesn't have that same texture and is unsuitable for making *tang yuan*. The amount of liquid you add to the flour varies depending on the brand and the humidity in the room. I usually start with ⅓ cup (90 ml) water, then slowly add more.

Makes 15

港式班戟

Peanut and Condensed Milk Pancakes

Time
15 minutes, plus 30 minutes resting

Ingredients
1½ cups (185 g) all-purpose flour
1½ tbsp custard powder (See Note)
2 tsp baking powder
1 tsp salt
2 eggs
¼ cup (50 g) sugar
about 1 cup (220–240 ml) milk
2¾ tbsp salted butter, melted

For the filling (per pancake)
1 tbsp crunchy peanut butter
2 tsp condensed milk

One of Hong Kong's most popular street snacks are egg waffles. Years ago, some of the street stalls sold a pancake version made with the same batter, but nowadays these old-school stalls are difficult to find. This is a simple recipe to make Hong Kong-style pancakes at home, served with the classic peanut butter and condensed milk combo. They taste just like they do on the busy streets of Hong Kong.

In a large bowl, whisk together the flour, custard powder, baking powder and salt.

In a medium bowl, whisk together the eggs, sugar, milk and melted butter. Add the dry ingredients to the wet and whisk until smooth. Leave to rest for at least 30 minutes.

Heat a nonstick frying pan over medium-low heat (no need to add any oil). Ladle 4–5 tablespoons of batter into the center of the pan (do not spread the batter with the spoon, let it naturally spread into a round pancake shape). Cook for 3–4 minutes, or until bubbles appear all over the top of the pancake. Flip and cook for a further 1–2 minutes (do not press the pancake down with the spatula, as this will flatten the pancake). Transfer to a plate and repeat with the remaining batter.

Spread each pancake with peanut butter and condensed milk, then fold in half. Serve immediately.

Note
Look for custard powder in the British or international foods aisle of most grocery stores.

芝麻饼干
Sesame Cookies

Time
30 minutes

Ingredients

1 stick (120 g) salted butter, softened

¾ cup (150 g) sugar (superfine if you have it)

1 tsp vanilla extract

1 egg, whisked

2 cups (240 g) all-purpose flour

1 tsp baking powder

½ tsp baking soda

1 tsp salt

⅓ cup (50 g) white and black sesame seeds, toasted

In a classic Hong Kong bakery, there is always a section in the back for cookies and treats. Often made with various nuts and seeds, these are traditionally given to friends and family as gifts. These sesame cookies are just like the ones they sell in these bakeries—crispy, nutty and perfect to enjoy with a fresh cup of tea.

In a large mixing bowl, beat the butter and sugar until smooth, around 3–5 minutes. Add the vanilla and egg, and mix to combine.

In a separate large bowl, whisk together the flour, baking powder, baking soda and salt. Add the flour to the butter mixture and mix to a smooth dough. Transfer to the fridge to chill for 15 minutes.

Meanwhile, preheat the oven to 350°F (180°C). Line a baking sheet with parchment paper. Place the sesame seeds onto a small plate.

Remove the dough from the fridge and divide it into 12 small balls, each about 1 tablespoon in size. Press each dough ball into a flat disc, around ¼ in (5 mm) thick. Gently lower one side of each disc into the sesame seeds and press to evenly coat. Transfer the cookies, seeded-side up, to the prepared baking sheet.

Bake for 8–10 minutes until golden and crisp, then transfer to a wire rack to cool. These are best enjoyed immediately while they are still super crispy.

杏仁饼
Almond Cookies

Time

30–35 minutes, plus 30 minutes chilling

Ingredients

11 tbsp (160 g) unsalted butter, softened

scant ½ cup (80 g) sugar (superfine if you have it)

4 egg yolks

½ tsp vanilla extract

¼ tsp salt

2½ cups (200 g) ground almonds

1 tsp baking powder

1 tsp baking soda

26 whole almonds

These almond cookies are inspired by those from a Hong Kong bakery specializing in artisanal cookies packaged in beautiful tin boxes—the type of boxes that my grandma has dotted all over her apartment. These nutty, crumbly cookies make wonderful presents to give to friends, family and colleagues. *Pictured overleaf.*

In a large mixing bowl, beat the butter and sugar until smooth, 3–5 minutes. Add the egg yolks and vanilla and mix to combine, then add the salt, ground almonds, baking powder and baking soda, and mix until combined. The dough should feel quite thick and tacky. Place the dough in the fridge to chill for at least 30 minutes.

Preheat the oven to 350°F (180°C). Line one or two baking sheets with parchment paper.

Divide the dough into about 26 balls, each about 1 tablespoon (20 g) in size. Place onto the prepared baking sheets, leaving about ¾ in (2 cm) distance between the cookies. With your forefingers, gently press the dough balls out into circles, about ½ in (1 cm) thick. Press an almond evenly into the center of each circle.

Bake the cookies for 16–18 minutes until golden and crisp, then transfer to a wire rack to cool. These are best enjoyed immediately while they're super crispy.

蛋撻
Cheater's Hong Kong-Style Egg Tart

Time
35–40 minutes

Ingredients

scant ½ cup (80 g) sugar

½ tsp salt

scant 1 cup (200 ml) boiling water

2 tbsp melted unsalted butter (or neutral cooking oil)

11 oz (320 g) ready-made puff pastry or shortcrust pastry (pie crust dough), chilled (see Note)

⅓ cup (80 g) evaporated milk (or substitute whole milk)

2 whole eggs, plus 2 egg yolks

2 tsp vanilla extract

Egg tarts are one of Hong Kong's most famous pastries. Different from Portuguese egg custard tarts, Hong Kong egg tarts have a light eggy filling and, in general, a thinner shortcrust pastry. One of my favorite afternoon snacks is a hot cup of Hong Kong milk tea and a freshly baked egg tart. This is my short-cut recipe that combines store-bought pastry with that signature, delicious, jelly-like egg custard in the middle.

Preheat the oven to 350°F (180°C).

Place the sugar and salt in a medium bowl and add the hot water. Mix and leave the sugar to dissolve and the water to cool.

Lightly brush a 12-hole muffin pan with melted butter or oil. With the rim of a large mug or a cookie cutter (around 3–3½ in/8–9 cm in diameter), cut the pastry into 12 circles. Cut a piece of parchment paper (use the paper the puff pastry comes rolled in, if possible) into 24 thin strips (each around 6 in/15 cm in length). Place two strips of paper in a cross shape on top of each circle of pastry, then gently press the pastry circles into each muffin cup, with the paper facing downwards. These strips will make it much easier to remove the tarts from the pan later on. Alternatively, you can use paper cupcake liners. Prick the base of each pastry circle with a fork. Bake for 10–12 minutes, or until light golden brown.

Meanwhile, in a medium bowl, whisk together the evaporated milk, whole eggs, egg yolks and vanilla extract until smooth.

Once the sugar-water mixture has cooled, whisk it into the egg mixture. Strain the mixture through a fine-mesh sieve into a jug, to remove any bubbles, and set aside.

Remove the par-baked tart shells from the oven. Divide the egg mixture evenly among the tart shells (leaving a ¼ in/5 mm gap at the top of each one). Return to the oven to bake for a further 18–20 minutes until the custard has set. It should still slightly jiggle in the center. Leave to cool for 5 minutes. These are best enjoyed warm.

Note
Depending on how your pastry is packaged, you may need to roll out your pastry or use more than one sheet.

花生雪糕
No-Churn Peanut Ice Cream

Time

15 minutes, plus
4-6 hours freezing

Ingredients

generous 1 cup (350 g) condensed milk

1 tsp vanilla extract

5 tbsp peanut butter (see Note)

2 cups (470 ml) heavy cream

2 tbsp peanuts, roughly chopped (optional)

This is a base recipe for an easy homemade no-churn ice cream with only three ingredients. I've made so many variations of this, stirring in fresh passion fruit, chopped strawberries, mango purée and even chocolate chips. I'm using peanut butter here, but feel free to use any nut butter you like.

In a large bowl, whisk together the condensed milk, vanilla extract and 3 tablespoons of the peanut butter until smooth.

In a separate large bowl, whip the cream to stiff peaks. Gently fold the whipped cream through the condensed milk mixture.

Transfer the mixture to an airtight container. Gently stir in the remaining 2 tablespoons of peanut butter to create a rippled effect, and sprinkle over the peanuts (if using). Place in the freezer for 4-6 hours until completely frozen.

This ice cream will keep for 2-3 months in the freezer.

Note

If using unsweetened nut butter, you might want to add some sugar to adjust for sweetness. If using sweetened nut butters, be aware that your ice cream will be on the sweeter side.

Variations:

Almond: Add 1 teaspoon of almond extract and swap peanut butter for almond butter and peanuts for almonds.

Orange: Skip the peanut ingredients. Add 1 teaspoon of orange extract, the zest of 1 orange, and stir in 2½ oz (70 g) candied orange peel.

Ginger: Skip the peanut ingredients. Add 2 tablespoons of ginger juice (grate a large piece of fresh ginger root and squeeze out the juice) and stir in 2½ oz (70 g) candied ginger, roughly chopped.

Mint Chocolate: Skip the peanut ingredients. Add 1-2 teaspoons of peppermint extract and stir in a generous ½ cup (100 g) chocolate chips or roughly chopped dark chocolate.

Rum and Raisin: Skip the peanut ingredients. Soak ½ cup (80 g) raisins in 4-6 tablespoons of rum for 20 minutes, then stir the rum and raisins into the ice cream base.

index

almonds
   almond cookies 207
   no-churn almond ice cream 213
asparagus: Fujian fried rice 117

bacon
   bacon and ketchup fried rice 57
   braised Chinese cabbage with smoked bacon 170
   steamed vegetable and bacon rice 48
bang bang shrimp 86
beansprouts
   beef chow fun 66
   chow mein 68
   cold sesame noodles 94
   crispy chicken noodles with gravy 51
   Hong Kong stir-fried noodles 65
   vegetable spring rolls 166–7
beef
   beef and broccoli stir-fry 69
   beef chow fun 66
   crispy chile beef 77
   Hong Kong-style beef gravy with rice 49
beer: red braised pork belly 104
black bean tofu 39
black rice vinegar 15
bok choi
   bok choi with soy gravy 157
   fried pork chop with soup noodles 52
   longevity noodles 107
   Shanghai stir-fried thick noodles 33
   simple soup noodles 98
   soy and vinegar mixed noodles 95
   steamed vegetable and bacon rice 48
   whole braised mushrooms 122
braised Chinese cabbage with smoked bacon 170
bread: shrimp toast 178
broccoli
   beef and broccoli stir-fry 69
   garlicky stir-fried broccoli 160

cabbage
   braised Chinese cabbage with smoked bacon 170
   chow mein 68
   easy rice cooker dinner 30
   hand-torn cabbage stir-fry 161
   pork and cabbage dumplings 146
   Shanghai stir-fried thick noodles 33
   vegetable spring rolls 166–7
Cantonese-style clay pot eggplant 114
carrots
   chow mein 68

easy rice cooker dinner 30
   Fujian fried rice 117
   vegetable spring rolls 166–7
char siu 132
cheater's Hong Kong-style egg tart 210
cheese: baked tomato pork chop with fried rice 113
chicken
   baked whole soy sauce chicken 131
   chicken and corn dumplings 150
   chicken and corn soup 31
   chicken clay pot rice 46
   crispy chicken noodles with gravy 51
   Fujian fried rice 117
   kung pao chicken 85
   lemon chicken 73
   steamed chicken and mushrooms 42
   white-cut chicken with ginger and scallion sauce 102
chile bean paste 14
   Cantonese-style clay pot eggplant 114
   mapo tofu 81
chiles
   basic chile oil 190
   crispy chile beef 77
   fresh chile and soy sauce 145
   hand-torn cabbage stir-fry 161
   kung pao chicken 85
   mapo tofu 81
   salt and pepper tofu 88
   simple steamed fish 110
   stuffed chile peppers 164
   typhoon shelter shrimp 119
Chinese cabbage with smoked bacon, braised 170
Chinese dining etiquette 22
Chinese sausage 15
   chicken clay pot rice 46
   easy rice cooker dinner 30
Chinese sesame paste 15
   dan dan noodles 78
chocolate ice cream, no-churn 213
chow mein 68
cilantro
   sesame crunch sauce 145
   simple steamed fish 110
coconut milk
   mango pomelo sago pudding 197
   mango sticky rice 194
condensed milk
   no-churn peanut ice cream 213
   peanut and condensed milk pancakes 203

cookies
   almond cookies 207
   sesame cookies 204
corn
   chicken and corn dumplings 150
   chicken and corn soup 31
cornstarch 12
cream: no-churn peanut ice cream 213
crispy chicken noodles with gravy 51
crispy chile beef 77
crispy garlic green beans 156
crispy tofu with spicy mushroom gravy 116
cucumber
   cold sesame noodles 94
   smacked cucumber salad 163

dan dan noodles 78
desserts 192–213
dining etiquette, Chinese 22
dipping sauces 164
   fresh chile and soy sauce 145
   sesame crunch sauce 145
   sour and spicy sauce 145
dumplings 136–40
   chicken and corn dumplings 150
   dumpling dough 140
   how to cook 144
   how to fold 142
   pork and cabbage dumplings 146
   sauces for 145
   tofu, mushroom and spinach dumplings 147

easy rice cooker dinner 30
eggs
   bacon and ketchup fried rice 57
   baked tomato pork chop with fried rice 113
   cheater's Hong Kong-style egg tart 210
   classic egg fried rice 55
   egg drop soup 74
   Fujian fried rice 117
   garlic fried rice 57
   not-so-classic egg fried rice 56
   pork chop with scallion sauce and rice 28
   shrimp and egg white fried rice 56
   soft-boiled tea eggs 173
   steamed egg 45
   tomato and egg stir-fry 38
eggplant, Cantonese-style clay pot 114
evaporated milk
   cheater's Hong Kong-style egg tart 210
   mango pomelo sago pudding 197

fish, simple steamed 110
Fujian fried rice 117

garlic
  beef and broccoli stir-fry 69
  crispy garlic green beans 156
  garlic fried rice 57
  garlicky stir-fried broccoli 160
  ginger and garlic stir-fried lettuce 171
  hand-torn cabbage stir-fry 161
  shrimp clay pot vermicelli 125
  stir-fried spicy garlic noodles 95
  sweet soy sauce 191
  typhoon shelter shrimp 119
ginger
  baked whole soy sauce chicken 131
  basic chile oil 190
  braised Chinese cabbage with smoked bacon 170
  Cantonese-style clay pot eggplant 114
  fried pork chop with soup noodles 52
  ginger and garlic stir-fried lettuce 171
  ginger and scallion sauce 187
  kung pao chicken 85
  no-churn ginger ice cream 213
  red braised pork belly 104
  shrimp clay pot vermicelli 125
  simple steamed fish 110
  steamed chicken and mushrooms 42
  sweet and sour pork ribs 128
  sweet soy sauce 191
  tang yuan in sweet ginger soup 198
  typhoon shelter shrimp 119
  white-cut chicken with ginger and scallion sauce 102
Grandma's boozy pork belly 108
gravy
  bok choi with soy gravy 157
  crispy chicken noodles with gravy 51
  spicy mushroom gravy 116
green beans, crispy garlic 156

hoisin sauce: char siu 132
Hong Kong stir-fried noodles 65
Hong Kong-style beef gravy with rice 49
hot and sour soup 91
hot and sour soup noodles 99

ice cream, no-churn peanut 213
ingredients 10–17

ketchup
  bacon and ketchup fried rice 57

baked tomato pork chop with fried rice 113
  ketchup shrimp 34
  sweet and sour pork 62
kung pao chicken 85

lemon chicken 73
lettuce, ginger and garlic stir-fried 171
longevity noodles 107

mango
  mango pomelo sago pudding 197
  mango sticky rice 194
mapo tofu 81
mushroom stir-fry sauce 12
mushrooms
  chicken clay pot rice 46
  crispy chicken noodles with gravy 51
  crispy tofu with spicy mushroom gravy 116
  dan dan noodles 78
  dried mushrooms 13
  hot and sour soup 91
  longevity noodles 107
  mapo tofu 81
  pork and woodear mushroom wontons 151
  Shanghai stir-fried thick noodles 33
  steamed chicken and mushrooms 42
  tofu, mushroom and spinach dumplings 147
  whole braised mushrooms 122

no-churn peanut ice cream 213
noodles
  beef chow fun 66
  chow mein 68
  cold sesame noodles 94
  cooking 65
  crispy chicken noodles with gravy 51
  dan dan noodles 78
  fried pork chop with soup noodles 52
  Hong Kong stir-fried noodles 65
  hot and sour soup noodles 99
  longevity noodles 107
  noodles 5 ways 93–9
  scallion oil noodles 26
  Shanghai stir-fried thick noodles 33
  shrimp clay pot vermicelli 125
  simple soup noodles 98
  soy and vinegar mixed noodles 95
  stir-fried spicy garlic noodles 95
  varieties of 16

oils
  basic chile oil 190
  sesame oil 11
orange ice cream, no-churn 213
oyster sauce 12
  char siu 132

pancakes
  peanut and condensed milk pancakes 203
  scallion pancakes 180
peanut butter
  no-churn peanut ice cream 213
  peanut and condensed milk pancakes 203
  tang yuan in sweet ginger soup 198
peanuts
  kung pao chicken 85
  tang yuan in sweet ginger soup 198
peas: Hong Kong-style beef gravy with rice 49
peppers
  black bean tofu 39
  crispy chile beef 77
  easy chile sauce 186
  stuffed chile peppers 164
  sweet and sour pork 62
pineapple
  baked tomato pork chop with fried rice 113
  sweet and sour pork 62
pomelo: mango pomelo sago pudding 197
pork
  baked tomato pork chop with fried rice 113
  char siu 132
  fried pork chop with soup noodles 52
  Grandma's boozy pork belly 108
  pork and cabbage dumplings 146
  pork and woodear mushroom wontons 151
  pork chop with scallion sauce and rice 28
  red braised pork belly 104
  sweet and sour pork 62
  sweet and sour pork ribs 128
puff pastry: cheater's Hong Kong-style egg tart 210

raisins: no-churn rum and raisin ice cream 213
red braised pork belly 104
rice
  bacon and ketchup fried rice 57

baked tomato pork chop with fried rice 113
chicken clay pot rice 46
classic egg fried rice 55
cooling rice 19
easy rice cooker dinner 30
fried rice 5 ways 55–7
Fujian fried rice 117
garlic fried rice 57
Hong Kong-style beef gravy with rice 49
how to cook perfect rice 18–19
mango sticky rice 194
not-so-classic egg fried rice 56
pork chop with scallion sauce and rice 28
shrimp and egg white fried rice 56
steamed vegetable and bacon rice 48
varieties of 17

rice flour: *tang yuan* in sweet ginger soup 198
rum and raisin ice cream, no-churn 213

sago pearls: mango pomelo sago pudding 197
salad, smacked cucumber 163
salt and pepper tofu 88
sauces
  easy chile sauce 186
  fresh chile and soy sauce 145
  ginger and scallion sauce 187
  sesame crunch sauce 145
  sour and spicy sauce 145
scallions
  bacon and ketchup fried rice 57
  beef chow fun 66
  chow mein 68
  classic egg fried rice 55
  fried pork chop with soup noodles 52
  garlic fried rice 57
  ginger and scallion sauce 187
  Hong Kong stir-fried noodles 65
  kung pao chicken 85
  longevity noodles 107
  mapo tofu 81
  not-so-classic egg fried rice 56
  pork chop with scallion sauce and rice 28
  red braised pork belly 104
  scallion oil noodles 26
  scallion pancakes 180
  shrimp and egg white fried rice 56
  shrimp clay pot vermicelli 125
  simple steamed fish 110
  sweet and sour pork ribs 128
  tomato and egg stir-fry 38
  white-cut chicken with ginger and scallion sauce 102

sesame oil 11
sesame paste
  cold sesame noodles 94
  sesame crunch sauce 145
sesame seeds
  sesame cookies 204
  shrimp toast 178
  smacked cucumber salad 163
shallot crisp 188
Shanghai stir-fried thick noodles 33
Shaoxing rice wine 12
shiitake mushrooms
  chicken clay pot rice 46
  crispy chicken noodles with gravy 51
  crispy tofu with spicy mushroom gravy 116
  dan dan noodles 78
  longevity noodles 107
  mapo tofu 81
  Shanghai stir-fried thick noodles 33
  steamed chicken and mushrooms 42
  tofu, mushroom and spinach dumplings 147
  whole braised mushrooms 122
shrimp
  bang bang shrimp 86
  Fujian fried rice 117
  ketchup shrimp 34
  shrimp and egg white fried rice 56
  shrimp clay pot vermicelli 125
  shrimp toast 178
  shrimp wontons 153
  stuffed chile peppers 164
  typhoon shelter shrimp 119
smacked cucumber salad 163
soup
  chicken and corn soup 31
  egg drop soup 74
  hot and sour soup 91
  hot and sour soup noodles 99
  simple soup noodles 98
  tang yuan in sweet ginger soup 198
sour and spicy sauce 145
soy sauce
  baked whole soy sauce chicken 131
  bok choi with soy gravy 157
  chilled soy tofu 175
  dark soy sauce 11
  light soy sauce 11
  shallot crisp 188
  soy and vinegar mixed noodles 95
  sweet soy sauce 191
spinach: tofu, mushroom and spinach dumplings 147
spring rolls, vegetable 166–7
Sriracha sauce: cold sesame noodles 94
steaming 20–1

stir-fries
  beef and broccoli stir-fry 69
  hand-torn cabbage stir-fry 161
  Hong Kong stir-fried noodles 65
  stir-fried spicy garlic noodles 95
  tomato and egg stir-fry 38
stuffed chile peppers 164
sweet and sour pork 62
  sweet and sour pork ribs 128
sweet soy sauce 191
  char siu 132
  pork chop with scallion sauce and rice 28

tang yuan in sweet ginger soup 198
tart, cheater's Hong Kong-style egg 210
tea eggs, soft-boiled 173
Thai sweet chile sauce
  bang bang shrimp 86
  crispy chile beef 77
  shrimp toast 178
  vegetable spring rolls 166–7
tofu
  black bean tofu 39
  chilled soy tofu 175
  crispy tofu with spicy mushroom gravy 116
  hot and sour soup 91
  mapo tofu 81
  salt and pepper tofu 88
  shrimp clay pot vermicelli 125
  tofu, mushroom and spinach dumplings 147
  varieties of 16
tomatoes
  baked tomato pork chop with fried rice 113
  ketchup shrimp 34
  tomato and egg stir-fry 38
typhoon shelter shrimp 119

vegetables
  steamed vegetable and bacon rice 48
  vegetable spring rolls 166–7
  see also individual types of vegetable

white-cut chicken with ginger and spring onion sauce 102
wontons
  how to cook 144
  how to fold 143
  pork and mushroom wontons 151
  shrimp wontons 153
  wonton dough 141

conversion tables

Recipes have been tested using metric measurements. Imperial conversions may yield different results. Follow one set of measurements only—do not mix metric and imperial.

Weight

Metric	Imperial
15 g	½ oz
25 g	1 oz
40 g	1½ oz
50 g	2 oz
75 g	3 oz
100 g	4 oz
150 g	5 oz
175 g	6 oz
200 g	7 oz
225 g	8 oz
250 g	9 oz
275 g	10 oz
350 g	12 oz
375 g	13 oz
400 g	14 oz
425 g	15 oz
450 g	1 lb
550 g	1¼ lb
675 g	1½ lb
900 g	2 lb
1.5 kg	3 lb

Volume

Metric	Imperial
25 ml	1 fl oz
60 ml	2 fl oz (¼ cup)
85 ml	3 fl oz
120 ml	4 fl oz (½ cup)
240 ml	1 cup
475 ml	2 cups
600 ml	2½ cups
700 ml	3 cups
950 ml	4 cups (1 quart)
1 liter	4¼ cups
1.2 liters	5 cups
1.25 liters	5¼ cups
1.5 liters	6⅓ cups
1.6 liters	6¾ cups
1.75 liters	7½ cups
2 liters	8½ cups (2 quarts)
2.25 liters	9½ cups
3 liters	12⅔ cups
3.75 liters	16 cups (1 gallon)
4 liters	17 cups

Measurements

Metric	Imperial
0.5 cm	¼ inch
1 cm	½ inch
2.5 cm	1 inch
5 cm	2 inches
10 cm	4 inches
15 cm	6 inches
18 cm	7 inches
20 cm	8 inches
23 cm	9 inches
25 cm	10 inches
30 cm	12 inches

Oven Temperatures

°C	°F
140°C	275°F
150°C	300°F
160°C	325°F
180°C	350°F
190°C	375°F
200°C	400°F
220°C	425°F
230°C	450°F
240°C	475°F

thanks

Thank you to everyone who helped me bring this book to life. Thank you to Ru, for giving me this opportunity and making my dream of publishing a cookbook come true. To Emily, for helping me through every stage of this book. To Ola, for the fearless recipe photography. Valerie, for being a kitchen wizard. To Amelia and Bonnie from Double Slice studio, for the amazing design and illustrations. Thank you to everyone else at Ebury who helped me along the way.

Thank you to my partner Egg, who took a leap of faith and moved from London to Hong Kong with me. No job, no plan—just a few suitcases and an open mind. He's responsible for all the Hong Kong city photography in this book, taken on film in various formats. He's a chef and baker, and gave me constant feedback on the recipes. Without him, this book wouldn't have happened. Thank you for constantly supporting and believing in me, no matter what I do. For being there when I'm doubting myself and for being there when I'm celebrating. I'm so grateful for you.

Thank you to my parents. Mom, Dad, you allowed me to explore all my passions and curiosities. Thank you for showing me the world and making me feel like I can do anything I want in it. Thank you to my extended family—my grandparents, aunts, uncles, cousins and Aunty Vicky. Without you all, I wouldn't love and appreciate food as much as I do, and have learned how to cook delicious meals from nothing.

Thank you to all my friends. Helen and Sabrina, you've never once questioned my ability to achieve what I set my mind to. You're there to open a bottle of wine when I want to rant. You're there to hand me a tissue when I want to cry. Thank you.

Thank you to all my followers and subscribers. Seeing how you relate to my stories is why I keep doing what I do. I could not have done this without your support. I shared my stories online with no idea of where it would take me. It's been an incredible and unpredictable ride and I'm excited to stay on it.

about the author

Emma Chung cooks and shares stories online. Brought up in Hong Kong, Emma lived in Shanghai before moving to London where she was a recipe editor for Mindful Chef and taught cookery classes at the highly regarded Jeremy Pang's School of Wok. In 2024, she moved back to Hong Kong to be closer to family, and continues to share videos and recipes from her life in the city. She can be found online on Instagram and TikTok @iam.chungry, and on Youtube @iamchungry.

First published in 2025 by
Interlink Books
An imprint of Interlink Publishing Group, Inc.
46 Crosby Street
Northampton, Massachusetts 01060
www.interlinkbooks.com

Published simultaneously in the United Kingdom
by Ebury Press, part of the Penguin Random House group of companies.

Copyright © Emma Chung 2025
Photography © Ola O. Smit 2025

All rights reserved. No part of this publication may be reproduced, stored in a retrieval system, or transmitted, in any form or by any means, electronic, mechanical, photocopying, recording or otherwise, without the prior written permission of the publishers.

Library of Congress Cataloging-in-Publication Data available
ISBN 978-1-62371-602-8

Editorial Director: Ru Merritt
Project Editor: Emily Preece-Morrison
American Edition Editor: Leyla Moushabeck
Design: Double Slice (Amelia Leuzzi and Bonnie Eichelberger)
Photographer: Ola O. Smit
Food Stylist: Valerie Berry
Prop Stylist: Jennifer Kay
Indexer: Vanessa Bird

Color origination by Altaimage Ltd
Printed and bound in Malaysia by Papercraft Sdn Bhd

Interlink Publishing is committed to a sustainable future for our business, our readers and our planet. This book is made from Forest Stewardship Council® certified paper.

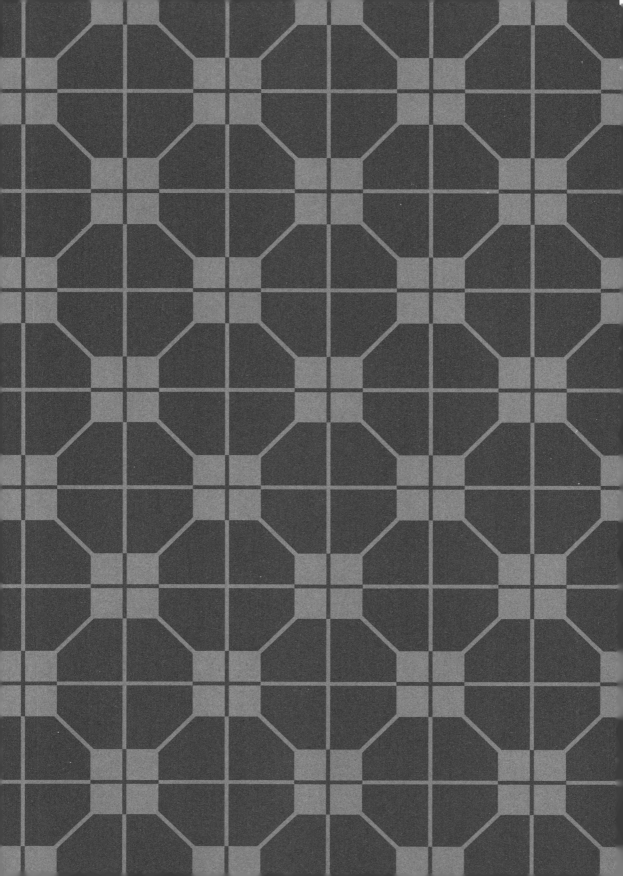